50 Ways to Stand Up for™ Your Family

*Build a Legacy of Love
for Everyday Living*

W. B. FREEMAN

STARBURST PUBLISHERS®

P.O. Box 4123, Lancaster, Pennsylvania 17604

To schedule author appearances, write:
Author Appearances
Starburst Promotions
P.O. Box 4123
Lancaster, PA 17604
or call 717-293-0939.

CREDITS:
Cover design by David Marty Design
Text design and composition by John Reinhardt Book Design

50 WAYS TO STAND UP FOR™ YOUR FAMILY
Copyright 2002 by Starburst Publishers, Inc.
All rights reserved.

This book may not be used or reproduced in any manner, in whole or in part, stored in a retrieval system or transmitted in any form by any means, electronic, mechanical, photocopy, recording, or otherwise, without written permission of the publisher, except as provided by USA copyright law.

First printing, October 2002
ISBN: 1-892016-74-5
Library of Congress Catalog Number: 2002107876
Printed in USA

Manuscript prepared by W. B. Freeman Concepts, Inc., Tulsa, Oklahoma.

Contents

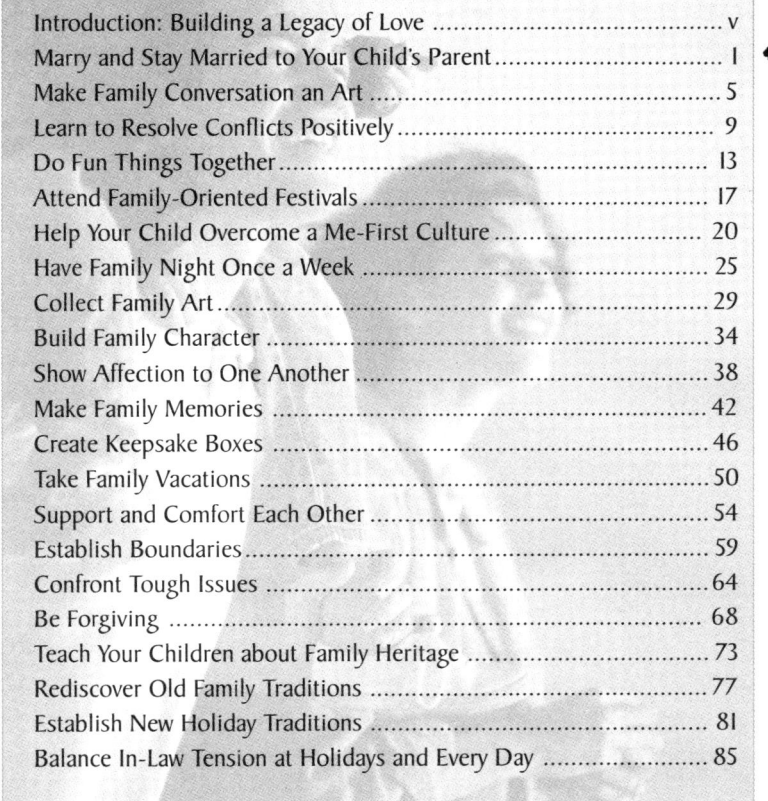

Introduction: Building a Legacy of Love v
Marry and Stay Married to Your Child's Parent 1
Make Family Conversation an Art 5
Learn to Resolve Conflicts Positively 9
Do Fun Things Together 13
Attend Family-Oriented Festivals 17
Help Your Child Overcome a Me-First Culture 20
Have Family Night Once a Week 25
Collect Family Art 29
Build Family Character 34
Show Affection to One Another 38
Make Family Memories 42
Create Keepsake Boxes 46
Take Family Vacations 50
Support and Comfort Each Other 54
Establish Boundaries 59
Confront Tough Issues 64
Be Forgiving 68
Teach Your Children about Family Heritage 73
Rediscover Old Family Traditions 77
Establish New Holiday Traditions 81
Balance In-Law Tension at Holidays and Every Day 85

Research Your Family Tree Together 90
Get Involved in Politics that Impact the Family 94
Get Involved in Your Child's School 99
Help Your Child Prepare for Higher Education 104
Read Together 109
Eat Together as Often as Possible 113
Visit Cities or Towns with Family Roots 117
Take Special Care of the Elderly in Your Family 120
Honor and Respect Elderly Members of Your Family 124
Correspond with Family Members 127
Date Your Spouse 132
Attend Family Events 136
Organize Family Reunions 140
Pray for Your Family 144
Pray with Your Family 147
Plant a Memorial Tree 150
Handle Money Wisely 153
Exercise Together 157
Volunteer Together 161
Create a Positive Family Atmosphere 165
Teach Children to Budget 169
Worship as a Family 173
Do Home Chores Together 177
Develop a Family Health and Safety Plan 182
Guard against Negative Influences 187
Schedule One-on-One Time 192
Redecorate Together 196
Be an Encourager 200
Nurture One Another's Talents 204

APPENDIX: A Reflective Test for Parents 209

INTRODUCTION: Building a Legacy of Love

You don't choose your family. They are God's gift to you, as you are to them.

—Archbishop Desmond Tutu

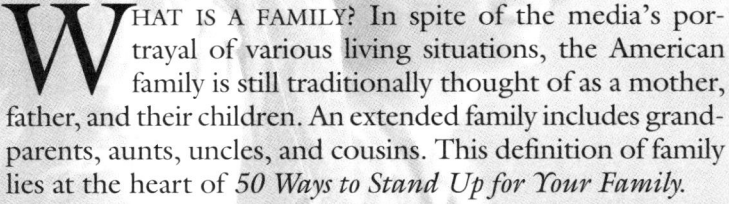

WHAT IS A FAMILY? In spite of the media's portrayal of various living situations, the American family is still traditionally thought of as a mother, father, and their children. An extended family includes grandparents, aunts, uncles, and cousins. This definition of family lies at the heart of *50 Ways to Stand Up for Your Family*.

While not all of today's families are living the ideal, we can still do our best to nurture the families we have. Divorce and other factors have made single parenthood a fact of life. Raising children alone is probably the hardest thing a parent will ever face. Parenting is a twenty-four-hour-a-day job, and doing it alone is not only physically and financially difficult, but also emotionally exhausting! We don't deny this challenge. This book seeks to support *all* parents.

The two-parent family is the foundation of American society, and the question we face today is how to make such a family stronger in our nation. America depends on healthy families to produce responsible citizens with respect for authority, social and financial responsibility, communication skills, and a strong value system.

Parents have tremendous responsibilities for their children:
- Teaching them skills and behaviors necessary for responsible, courteous, healthy, adulthood.
- Providing life's necessities, including food, clothing, and shelter, as well as proper emotional, intellectual, and spiritual resources.
- Nurture and love—giving abundant affection and appreciation, which aids the development of feelings of self-worth.
- Disciplining them to create an awareness of boundaries and the development of abiding respect for people and property.

The family is the basic unit for all cultures, the building block upon which children learn the do's and don'ts of getting along with others. Families teach children to be productive and reflect the positive aspects of their culture. Families also protect children from harm until they are old enough to support themselves. Even as adults, we never outgrow our need to receive *emotional* support from our families.

Regardless of the makeup of your family, you can create a home life that provides encouragement and solace, advice and instruction, safety and nurture. Your home can be the place of greatest fun, happiest memories, and the strongest bonds of love for your family.

The fifty topics covered in this book have practical applications. They are things an average parent or grandparent can do. Most of the ideas can be implemented with little expense and relatively few hours per month or year.

Regardless of your religious preference, cultural background, or political persuasion, you can profit from the fifty topics. All that is required to implement the suggestions we offer is a basic love for your family and a desire to see it endure beyond your lifetime.

Some of the ideas involve ways in which you and your family can interact more effectively with other elements of society. Every family is invariably linked to schools, neighborhoods, stores, jobs, and places of worship.

Interaction is a two-way street. The family is strengthened by strong schools, neighborhoods, businesses, and places of worship. In turn, a strong family bolsters its surrounding schools, neighborhood, local business community, and place of worship. Many of the chapters in this book encourage you to draw from the resources around you, and in turn become involved in strengthening resources that benefit our whole society.

By strengthening your family you are not only preparing your child for success but also defining the future for us all.

—W. B. Freeman

1 Marry and Stay Married to Your Child's Parent

Make a conscious decision each morning: "Today I will love my partner and my kids to the best of my ability."

—JAY STRACK

THE FOREMOST WAY to stand up for your family is to marry and stay married to the parent of your child. The security of a loving and stable family—with both Mom and Dad present in the home as caregivers and authority figures—is vital to a child's feeling of stability, development toward maturity, success in school, and ability to build healthy relationships.

Parenting is a two-person job! Fathers have distinct input into a child's life, as do mothers. Parenting calls for two-person agreement. Throughout history, legal precedent and truthful testimony have been established by the agreement of two witnesses. In a family, Mom and Dad function as "two witnesses" to a child—speaking the same message and conveying the same love, although perhaps using different words and methods of expression. Together mothers and fathers give their children the only two lasting possessions a child takes from a home: a value system and a belief system.

Value Your Marriage and Family

Here are five suggestions for valuing your marriage and family:

1. See your spouse as a valued and beloved child of God, and attempt to treat your spouse as you know God desires for him or her to be treated.

2. See your family as God's gift to you. Every child is a blessing that God expects you to cherish. Never regard your child as a burden. Your child will detect such an attitude even if you do not intend to convey that feeling.

3. See yourself as being accountable to God for the way you treat your children. Accept your responsibilities as a parent and become a positive role model. Recognize that you are God with arms, eyes, and heart to your child.

4. Love your spouse and your children unconditionally, with a quickness to forgive, show mercy, and voice appreciation and praise.

5. Acknowledge that the way you see your spouse, children, and yourself is a choice of your will. You *choose* to love and value your family members.

Make Family a Priority

It is interesting to note the criteria that a court system uses in determining guardianship for a child. Under the overall banner of "the best interests of the child," these six factors are evaluated:[1]

1. Has a living pattern been established for the child—associations with a community, school, and religious group—that promotes continuity and stability?

2. Have emotional ties been established that help the child counter day-to-day fears and express day-to-day hopes?

3. Is the child's home environment conducive to good physical health and safety? Are the child's needs for food, clothing, shelter, and medical care being met?

4. Is a plan in place to provide for the child's education, including higher education?

5. Does the parent behave circumspectly and morally, and have regular religious involvement? (Adultery and promiscuity factor significantly into custody conflicts, as do use of drugs and alcohol, and misappropriation of money.)

6. Does a parent express hatred, disregard, disfavor, or ongoing acrimony toward another parent?

These are good questions for parents to ask about their own marriage and family life, even if no thought of separation or divorce is under consideration.

The Impact of Divorce on Children

According to Laurene Johnson and Georglyn Rosenfeld, authors of *Divorced Kids*, children of divorced parents routinely experience sadness, feelings of abandonment and isolation, confusion and disorientation, a feeling of being torn between parents, forced adulthood, codependency, feelings of being overly burdened, and residual feelings of anger.[2]

Research has consistently shown that if a child is experiencing turmoil in his heart or mind, his ability to learn is reduced as much as 90 percent. A study of 4,000 seven-year-olds revealed that chronic stress resulted in not only lower grades but also lower IQ scores.

Benefits of Marriage

A number of benefits of marriage have been noted in research conducted by psychologists and sociologists:

- People live longer if they are married, particularly if they are in good, satisfying relationships.
- Married people experience fewer depressive episodes, anxiety disorders, psychoses, post-traumatic stress disorders, and phobias than single or divorced people.
- Married people are less likely to be injured in accidents.
- A married man with heart disease is expected to live an average of four years longer than an unmarried man with a healthy heart.

The benefits are not only for those who are married but also for the children in a family.

- Children in a home where Dad and Mom love each other have a greater sense of security than do children in a single-parent home.
- Children in two-parent homes tend to have greater trust in their caregivers, form attachments more easily, express affection more readily, are greater givers, and adjust more easily to changes.

Children in a happy two-parent home exude a "feeling of rightness, the basis for strong self-esteem" according to pediatrician and professor of pediatrics William Sears, M.D.

2 Make Family Conversation an Art

A good listener is not only popular everywhere, but after a while he gets to know something.

—WILSON MIZNER

"ENCOURAGE YOUR CHILD to talk and talk," says Dr. Susan Smith Kuczmarski, author of *The Family Bond*. She tells parents to be "open, direct, and deep" in talking with their child to "create rich and rare friendships."[1]

Good family communication begins long before a child is conceived. Communication between parents directly affects the mood of a pregnant mother, which in turn can impact a child's development. Families that bond through good communication generally find they build trust and loyalty that can't be replicated by any other means!

Rules of Good Conversation

The rules of good conversation are not much different in a family than in any social situation:
- Show genuine interest in the other person.
- Pay attention and don't interrupt.
- Empathize with how the other person is feeling.
- Respond both verbally and nonverbally.
- Be yourself.
- Listen, listen, listen.

Stages of Development

Adapt your conversation to the developmental stage of your child. Even when he or she is an infant, respond through sounds or gestures as your child babbles, and make an attempt to talk to your child. Speak to your son or daughter as you work or help him or her—for example, while giving a bath or preparing food.

Kathryn Hirsh-Pasek, coauthor of *How Babies Talk*, suggests that as children learn to talk, parents let the child take the lead in the conversation and then build on his or her interests.[2] Don't finish sentences or fill silences when there are lapses in the conversation.

As a child grows older, the Golden Rule is a good guideline for conversation: Talk to your child as you would like someone to talk to you. Like adults, children don't want to be talked down to or ignored, even when a subject is beyond their understanding. Find ways to involve your child in some aspect of the discussion.

Adult Conversations

Children who spend time in the company of adults develop better conversation skills. If children are kept out of all adult conversations, they miss an opportunity to learn from good examples. A study published by Peter Benson reported that "almost 20 percent of sixth through twelfth graders have not had a good conversation lasting for at least ten minutes with at least one of their parents in more than a month."[3] Make it a practice to try to talk *at length* with your children on a regular basis.

Talk about Everything

Encourage a child to talk about everything. That way when the time comes for difficult or awkward conversations the pattern for good communication, understanding, and mutual respect will already be in place. By expressing your ideas, needs, feelings, and expectations, your child becomes comfortable with sharing his ideas, opinions, dreams, hopes, and emotions.

Although not everything is appropriate for group discussion, there shouldn't be any topic that is off limits for you and your child. If a child knows enough to ask questions or wants to enter unexplored territory, let him know you are the person he can safely ask or with whom he can discuss options and possibilities. Don't avoid topics just because they make you uncomfortable. Choose to be the one to answer your child's questions appropriately and with accurate information and sensitivity. At the same time, you have the privilege to answer questions about your personal past only to the degree you feel comfortable or believe answers are warranted.

Tennis Ball Conversation

As your child moves into his adolescent years and starts to limit responses to one-word answers, you may want to give a lesson that Dr. James Dobson taught his children. In his book

Coming Home, Dobson writes about how he taught his children conversation skills using tennis balls as a teaching device. (He attributes the idea to an article by Sybil Ferguson in *Woman's Day* magazine.)

Give your teenager three tennis balls and ask him to throw them to you one at a time. As you catch the balls, instead of returning them, simply hold onto them. Your teenager will wonder what sort of game this is. The fact is, it isn't much of a game—and it certainly isn't fun. The point? A good conversationalist throws the ball back.

Table Talk

Encourage conversation at the dinner table, with everyone taking part. If there is a lull in the table talk, have a few conversation starters in mind to strike up a discussion with your children. For example, ask such things as "What makes you laugh?" "What makes your best friend your best friend?" "What is something that bugs you?" Besides learning to express themselves, your children will know they are valued when you take a sincere interest in what they are thinking about.

Dinnertime at the home of Joseph and Rose Kennedy was a time when the entire family discussed history and current affairs. Robert Kennedy once noted, "I can hardly remember a mealtime, when the conversation was not dominated by what Franklin D. Roosevelt was doing or what was happening in the world."[4] Kennedy regarded the family dinner discussions as important to his education as his formal academic training.

The importance of family conversation is summed up succinctly by educator Susan Kuczmarski, who says, "Talk often and about everything!"[5]

3 Learn to Resolve Conflicts Positively

Good marriages are built on respectful disagreement and back-and-forth cooperation. We learn to cue each other, fill in for each other, forgive each other's fumbles, celebrate small victories. We revel in the realization that we're working on something bigger than both of us, and that parenthood is not only incredibly challenging but also incredibly enriching.

—Susan Lapinski

EFFECTIVE CONFLICT RESOLUTION in a family always begins with the marital relationship. Children learn how things get settled by watching their parents. Children may occasionally model behaviors they see in friends, other adults, or the media, but they understand that the house rules for conflicts are ultimately those of their parents. Consequently, don't expect your children to adhere to rules of fair play that you don't embrace fully!

The basic requirements for conflict resolution are few, but vital:
- Develop the ability to step back from a conflict and see it objectively.
- Value a relationship enough to resolve differences that threaten to destroy it.
- Learn to listen.
- Learn to paraphrase.
- Take responsibility for your own feelings and behavior.

A Learned Skill

Learning to deal with conflict is not a natural skill. Most people need information, coaching, and practice.

Young couples may benefit from developing a relationship with a mentor couple that has been married for many years and has mastered the art of conflict resolution in their own marriage.

Conflicts between children usually require an adult mediator. As children realize the sense of personal power that comes with effectively resolving conflicts, they become their own peacemakers and ultimately can become catalysts for conflict resolution between others.

Four Common Aspects

Conflict management has become an area of specialization in corporations, schools, and consulting agencies. A number of methods have developed, all of which have these four basic steps:

1. *Cool down.* Those involved in the conflict need to take a break, calm their anger, and get their thoughts together.

2. *Use "I" messages to start a discussion.* One person begins by saying, "I feel _____ (explain your emotions) when _____

(tell the person exactly what brought about this response in you). I want _____ (say what you want from the other person)."

For example, "I feel frustrated when you ignore me. I want you to listen to me when I'm talking to you." Or, "I feel sad when you call me names. I want you to stop calling me names."

Then, the person who was listening paraphrases what was said: "You feel. . . ."

These two steps are done twice so that each person gets an opportunity to explain his or her side of the conflict.

3. *Brainstorm.* Those involved come up with ideas to help solve their own problem. This is a chance for conflicting parties to become allies. Make a list of "we" ideas. For example, "We will always look at one another when one of us begins to speak."

4. *Agree.* Both parties must agree to the "we" ideas and give each other a positive sign of acceptance such as shaking hands, sharing a high five, or hugging. Behaviorists believe this ending step is very important to let those involved know that they are done, it's over, and things are okay.

Ten Tips

The Conflict Center (www.conflictcenter.org) in Denver, Colorado, offers ten tips to ease tension and work toward resolution:

- Respect everyone's ideas and needs.
- Listen so people will talk, and talk so people will listen.
- Turn problems into possibilities.
- Focus on the problem, not the person.
- Build power *with* not power *over* others.
- Express feelings without blaming others.
- Own your part of the conflict.

- Strategize to reach mutually agreeable solutions.
- Create options. One "right way" always creates losers.
- Solve the problem and build the relationship.

Matching Helps Set the Tone

How we communicate in conflicts can affect the outcome. Sometimes when people are embroiled in conflict they talk quickly, loudly, and all at once. As the volume gets higher, the amount communicated often decreases and slows down resolution. You can encourage a more civil disagreement by lowering your voice. When a person talks in a soft tone, the other party will most likely lower his or her voice to match. Matching works as long as both individuals are not angry to the point of becoming irrational. Slowing down the communication entails taking the time to listen. Listening is *not* waiting until the other person is finished speaking so you can begin. Listening is the art of understanding the other person's perspective.

Resolution is always easier if both people can avoid becoming defensive. Remember that not all disagreements are destructive; they become destructive when one or both sides wants to win more than they want resolution.

Resolution Is Good for Your Health

Effectively resolving family conflicts isn't just a matter of household peace, it is also a health issue. In a study reported in the medical journal *Psychosomatic Medicine,* researchers found a dramatic link between physical health and marital conflict. The more negative or hostile the behavior, the greater the negative effects on the immune system, increasing vulnerability to colds, heart disease, and cancer.[1]

4 Do Fun Things Together

We believed in our idea—a family park where parents and children could have fun together.

—WALT DISNEY

OVER-SCHEDULED CALENDARS seem to exert a centrifugal force on today's active families as they pull moms, dads, and kids in different directions. Balancing work and family time challenges a two-career family, not to mention taxing parent schedules to accommodate a child's practices, lessons, sports, work, and academics. In the midst of the chaos, families often leave one essential thing off their schedules—having fun together!

Family Night Out

Rule number one in family entertainment is this: Turn off the television! Watching television should be a rare exception, not a standard practice. Find creative and adventurous possibilities by exploring alternatives to television, and especially take a look beyond the routine to find fun in family-friendly settings.

Plan a regular family night out and give each person in the family an opportunity to select his or her favorite event for everyone to do together. First, establish some general guidelines regarding budget, suitability for all family members, and time frame—for example, no late hours on school and work nights. Check out library or newspaper listings for events in your town or city. Consider both indoor and outdoor events, spectator and participation sports, and educational and recreational activities.

Live Performances

Cultural events such as the theater or an orchestra concert are a learning experience for children who have never been to a live drama or symphony performance. Consult the newspaper's entertainment section for productions that are appropriate for your children. Many towns and most cities have children's theater productions and concerts geared specifically for youngsters.

Prepare your children to appreciate what they are going to see or hear. Before attending a symphony concert, you might find a recording of the music at the library and help your children learn what to listen for during the concert. Ask questions like "How does this music make you feel?" "What colors does this music make you think of?" "How would you describe the music to someone else—is it loud or soft, fast or slow?" "What instruments did you hear?" Your children will get far more out of a concert if they are prepared for the experience.

If you are taking your child to a performance of a well-known story, consider reading the story in advance as a family. If you can get a copy of the play, assign parts and do a family read-through prior to attending.

Root for the Home Team

Sports events are always fun for families, and they don't have to be expensive. Support your hometown team or become a fan of a local college team. When it comes to sports, be participants and not just spectators. Go bowling, ice skating, roller skating, golfing, fishing, skiing, or bicycling! Rent the equipment you'll need for a trial run before investing in expensive sports items. If you decide to buy, some stores sell good used equipment at significant cost savings.

Outdoor Fun

Outdoor nature activities are beneficial and educational for the whole family. Start a collection of unique rocks from hiking or rappelling outings. Research the geological history of the area to find out the ages and types of the rocks. At a nearby beach or seashore collect unusual shells and research the kind of sea creature that once lived in that shell.

Live Animals

Zoos and aquariums are a great way for children to observe live animals they have never seen. A guided walk through a local nature preserve provides opportunity to see birds and animals in their natural habitat.

You don't have to leave home to enjoy bird watching. Identify birds that are native to your area, and start feeding birds that live in your yard. The birds will depend on the food you provide, so be reliable in keeping a birdfeeder filled.

Wave a Flag

Summertime parades and picnics make for great family outings. Memorial Day parades and Fourth of July fireworks are fun for the whole family. Pack picnic food, insect repellent, sunglasses, and lawn chairs, and load up the car to wave a flag and watch a parade. Summer is also the season for county or state fairs. Besides riding the Ferris wheel and roller coaster, check out the exhibits of woodworking, homemade quilts, and canned goods. See how well you do judging cattle and livestock, and then match your picks with the decisions of the professionals.

Spontaneous Fun

Be spontaneous—dance with each other; sing loudly together; lie on your back and watch the clouds float by in different shapes; watch the sunset together; play one-on-one basketball; go to an outdoor concert.

It doesn't take a lot of time to plan family entertainment, but you have to decide to do it. Having fun keeps families together!

5 Attend Family-Oriented Festivals

Of journeying the benefits are many: the freshness it bringeth to the heart, the seeing and hearing of marvelous things, the delight of beholding new cities, the meeting of unknown friends, and the learning of high manners.

—SADI GULISTAN

SUMMER FESTIVALS ARE FUN and often educational. From medieval pageantry, bird and dog shows, Mozart to country music—festivals appeal to enthusiasts of all kinds. If your family has a special interest, such as art, antiques, or the environment, you will no doubt find a festival that suits you. If you already have your family vacation planned, check sources for a festival closer to home to enjoy on a weekend, or check the area where you are vacationing to see if a festival is planned there.

Regional Summer Festivals

Some large cities host festivals all summer long. In its stunningly beautiful location, Vancouver, British Columbia, has a natural appeal to vacationers. Known as the City of Summer Festivals, Vancouver's fare of family fun includes festivals for lovers of jazz, chamber, folk, and new music. There is also an annual children's festival that features theater, music, dance, puppetry, storytelling, and comedy from around the world.

Cross over the U.S. border and continue the festival tour in Seattle. Early in the season (April) you have an opportunity to see the city in cherry blossom bloom. That, along with a Japanese Cultural Festival, can be an unforgettable springtime adventure. In May, Seattle visitors can take in the children's festival, an international film festival, and the Northwest folk life festival. The Seattle children's festival is billed as the "largest performing arts festival for families in the United States." It is recommended for school groups or families as a celebration of world cultures.

In the Midwest, plan your family vacation time to include stops in Chicago, St. Louis, or Milwaukee to enjoy Heartland festivals. If your vacation is near the Chicago area, find time for a family bike ride along the lakefront and a stop at the Taste of Chicago festival of international foods, held annually at Navy Pier. In the evening take in the outdoor Grant Park concert in downtown Chicago.

After a visit to Six Flags and the Gateway Arch in St. Louis, take the family to the downtown Storytelling Festival or the English Country Faire at the Botanical Gardens.

Throughout the summer, Milwaukee tourists join residents to enjoy Irish, German, and Italian fairs that celebrate the city's rich ethnic population.

Chautauqua History

Travel in the northeast might take you to New York for a stop in Chautauqua. For more than a century, residents and visitors there have attended a famed series of outdoor lectures, a precursor to summer festivals. The historic Chautauqua movement began in the summer of 1874 to provide instruction for Sunday school teachers. It grew to become a school of languages, summer school for teachers, and a school of theology. It expanded to include more opportunities for all family members with clubs for young people in reading, music, fine arts, physical education, and religion. The movement caught on in states across the nation and has seen a recent revival with Chautauqua festivals in many states.

Festivals for Every Interest

Every region in the nation offers its own specialty festivals. Many are music festivals. Others are ethnic celebrations that provide an international flavor of the American community through foods, music, dance, and pageantry. Asian, African, South American, Caribbean, Mexican, Polish, Norwegian, Irish, German, Scottish, Celtic, Native American, Appalachian, and American folk festivals provide a way for children and adults to experience some of their cultural heritage.

If that's not enough, you'll find antique car shows, arts and crafts fairs, Renaissance life festivals, pet shows, kite and toy festivals, herb and harvest festivals, chili cook-offs, Shakespeare and film festivals, azalea festivals, May Day celebrations, Octoberfests, and River fests. If your family has a special interest, do some research on the internet and you'll be sure to find a summer festival to satisfy everyone.

Summer festivals are a popular and affordable form of family entertainment—that means they attract crowds. Be sure to book reservations far in advance to secure good accommodations.

Help Your Child Overcome a Me-First Culture

[People] have something invested in being nice people, and it's only when you have children that you realize you're not a nice person at all, but generally a selfish bully.

—Fay Weldon

A FAMILY ADVICE COLUMNIST recently received a letter from a mother who described her children as "sharing-impaired."

Raising unselfish children in a me-first, look-out-for-number-one society is difficult, especially with our emphasis on personal independence and individualism. While society gives lip service to generosity and sharing, it often demonstrates some things that are downright selfish. Television, movies, video games, and even some school activities encourage youngsters to put themselves first in every situation. Parents sometimes encourage their children to do whatever it takes to win a competitive contest. The result, although often not intended, is a snuffing out of a child's inclination to help others, give their best effort to a team, or do what's right for the good of all.

As an infant, a child is the center of his or her own universe. As the child grows, he or she learns that there are others in the world who have wants and needs of their own. One of the earliest socialization skills is sharing.

Parents Must Teach Unselfish Behaviors

The simple truth is that if you want your children to be unselfish, you're responsible for showing them how it's done.

Author Sharon Merhalski tells how she made unselfishness a tradition in her home.[1] From the time her children were very young, she made sure their friends felt welcome in her home. She set aside personal time to join them in play and really listen to them when they talked. The family often unofficially adopted kids whose own home lives were not nurturing or who needed guidance and a sense of belonging. Her children became accustomed to sharing space, possessions, and parents with friends whom they accepted as members of the family.

There are two important aspects to helping your children grow up with the understanding that they have a responsibility to society:

1. Model unselfishness and a volunteer spirit from the time your children are born. Find opportunities to tell them why what you are doing is important and makes you feel happy, rewarded, and connected to others. Help children be aware of the unselfish acts of other children. For example, tell them the story of twelve-year-old Jarrett, a Kentuckian who has been in cancer treatment since he was six. Wanting to cheer

up the children he met during months of hospitalization, he began a "Joy Cart" of stuffed animals to give to other hospitalized kids. Jarrett's Joy Carts are now in children's hospital wards across the United States, and Jarrett is still the chief fund-raiser for the project despite the fact that he is now wheelchair-bound.

2. Help your children identify situations in which they can do unselfish deeds. For example, you might say something like, "Since Alyson doesn't have a dad now, would you like to ask her to sit with you and Daddy at the Father-Daughter banquet?" To the best of your ability, encourage and facilitate individual volunteer activities that are appropriate for your children.

Point Out the Benefits of Sharing

Forcing a child to behave unselfishly can backfire if the child perceives that giving causes loss or pain. When a small child refuses to share, express disappointment and then engineer an opportunity to happily share in his place. Let him see you *enjoy* giving. Tell your child how giving or sharing makes you feel. Older children and teens often become unselfish volunteers if they learn about the people they are helping, the needs they are facing, and why they are facing those needs.

For example, John planned a weekend trip for his family to participate in the cleanup of a trash dump in the Appalachian foothills. Ned, his thirteen-year-old son, was less than enchanted by the prospect of spending the whole weekend with his parents and little sister picking up trash! Ned's parents agreed that he would not have to go if he would do a web search to help the rest of the family prepare for the trip.

He was assigned to find out all he could about the area, who lived there, and what was happening to the water supply and natural habitat because of the trash dump. At dinner the next night, he reported what he found. Among other things, Ned discovered that kids his age were getting sick because chemicals from the dump were filtering into their water. He also discovered that a lot of teens and college kids participated in cleanup weekends and thought they were fun. After Ned's almost enthusiastic report, the family agreed that if he would like to reconsider and go with them after all, they would cut the trip short by a day, unless Ned decided *he* wanted to stay. The end of this story? Ned has become a volunteer recruiter and leader at his school!

Part of Your Family's Identity

Syndicated columnist Jana Fortner advises elevating sharing to a cornerstone of your family's identity: "This is who we are—people who love each other enough to share."[2] There are many ways to become a family that shares.

- Make it the responsibility of younger children to sort the recyclables.
- Adopt a needy family for Thanksgiving. Pack a basket with a turkey and all the trimmings ready to cook, or invite the family to join yours at the table.
- Decorate a plastic jar and label it, "Change Our World." Each week challenge your children to do a sweep of the house looking for spare change for the jar. When it is full, take it to a supermarket counting machine, and then donate the money to charity.
- Instead of *buying* gifts for each other at Christmas, agree to make homemade gifts for family members and spend the gift money on presents for children on your local Angel Tree (or other toy donation program).
- Form a family clown troupe. Paint your faces, don old,

ugly, badly fitting clothes, and buy a bouquet of helium-filled balloons to entertain children at a local hospital. Spend time as a family rehearsing the silliest jokes and easiest magic tricks you can find.

• Adopt a grandparent (or three or four) at a local nursing home and have family dinner with them at the home once a month, or drop in weekly with a bag of cookies, child-crafted gifts, or flowers from your garden.

A Reward?

Should you reward children for volunteering or doing unselfish deeds? The answer is yes. The reward does not need to be monetary or tangible. It can be a hearty "Thank you" or a statement of admiration. Children need to know their parents are proud of them—praise is an important behavior-reinforcing tool at any age.

Think Long Term

Like most things in life, there is no quick fix for self-centeredness. Helping your child become an unselfish person takes time, patience, and creativity. Don't get discouraged. Keep trying to motivate your child to volunteer and develop compassion and mercy. With your guidance, one day they'll intuitively help others and make their community a healthier place to live.

> NOTE: *All access to the internet for children under eighteen years of age should be parentally controlled either through the presence of an adult or via internet service provider settings.*

7 Have Family Night Once a Week

The best things you can give children, next to good habits, are good memories.

—SYDNEY HARRIS

AT LEAST ONE CITY in our nation has officially recognized the importance of family time. In March of 2002, Ridgewood, New Jersey, designated one night as family night. The city council, in cooperation with the local school district, intended to create one evening in the city in which no outside activities might pull family members outside their homes—no homework was given, no city-sponsored meetings were scheduled, and no school-related rehearsals, sporting practices, or events were held. The intent was to allow families to spend an evening together at home.

What was rather amazing to many observers was that it took the school and civic leaders of Ridgewood seven months to find one night that could be set aside for family only. In an interview on *Good Morning America*, one educator observed, "We all have so much going on, it was difficult to find a night that could be cleared."

Many parents can relate to this abundance of activities on the family calendar. One recent survey estimated that today's average child has 25 percent fewer unstructured hours of nonschool time Monday through Friday than a child of two decades ago. A typical child has at least one extracurricular activity every school day of the year. Sports practices, band and drama rehearsals, clubs, part-time jobs, and music lessons are just a few possibilities.

Tips for Carving Out Family Time

Setting aside family time requires active participation from all family members, but the primary responsibility belongs to the parents.

- *Set aside a "family night" once a week.* It need not always be the same night. You may need to have a family meeting once a month to look at calendars and determine which nights can be set aside, free of any outside commitment, event, or meeting.

- *Limit child activities.* Put a cap on the number of sports your children play, the number of clubs to which you or your children belong, and the number of organizations you serve as a volunteer. Also limit the hours your child is allowed to work in a part-time job.

- *Control your work schedule.* Many parents today, especially those in their twenties and early thirties, seem to believe they are *expected* to work ten- to fourteen-hour days to appear committed to their employers. You may have to choose between a job that requires all your time and energy, and a less-demanding position (and perhaps less money) that allows you to spend more time with family. If faced with such a choice, choose family! Those who do so are often pleasantly surprised to discover how easily they adjust to a smaller salary, especially since they are spending more time with their children and thus need fewer babysitters, spend less money on expensive entertainment, and are rarely required to eat dinners away from home.

If you can't find an entire evening, at least find one leisurely meal you can eat together—perhaps Friday or Sunday night dinner, or Sunday lunch.

Defining Your Own Family Night

No two family members are exactly alike, so no two family nights are going to be the same. Here are some options:

- Spend family night at home, sharing a meal that you all help prepare. Then allow each person to go about his or her own reading or studying.
- Watch a family-friendly video together, sharing a giant tub of popcorn.
- Spend extra time at the dinner table in conversation. Family nights are an ideal time to pursue family hobbies, activities, or to plan upcoming vacations or events.
- Play board games or work a jigsaw puzzle together.
- Take a lesson together, perhaps learning gourmet cooking techniques via a video teacher. If you pursue this option, be sure to do something in which family members can talk, laugh, and work *together* at a task.
- Have a family talent night with each person contributing a song, story, or skit. If you'd like, invite grandparents or aunts, uncles, and cousins to join in.
- Read aloud a classic play, assigning each family member a part, or sing songs together in harmony around a piano.

As much as possible, keep the pace slow and the atmosphere low-key. Unless it is absolutely imperative that you be available for phone calls, unplug the phone or turn off the ringer. Make this night an oasis of peace in an otherwise busy week. Choose soothing music, turn off the TV, avoid the computer (and computer games), and say no to activities that isolate family members. If all members of the family are in a room reading or studying together, opportunity should be given for a person to ask a question of the group or share a tidbit of interesting information.

28. Learn to Say No

One of the best lessons you can teach your child is to say no to too many commitments. Teach your child that he or she can be involved in many things throughout life, but that it is best not to be overly involved in too many things at one time. That's a surefire formula for stress! While it may be nice to be invited into a club or organization, it is also acceptable to say, "I don't think I should take that on right now." No explanations or excuses are required.

8 Collect Family Art

All photographs are there to remind us of what we forget.

—John Berger

FAMILY PHOTOS. They're piled in boxes or stuck by corners in hefty albums—some old, some long forgotten, some curling at the edges from age, and *all* seldom seen. Even so, those whose homes and possessions have been destroyed by fire or flood often lament that the loss of these seldom-seen pieces of paper is more painful than the loss of any other possession.

Building an art gallery—or an organized collection of family photos, children's drawings, old postcards, and other visual memorabilia—is one way for children to discover that they are part of a family that extends beyond their house and generation. From preschool on, children can grasp the significance of relationship and see the physical resemblance between members of their family. Creating a family gallery can help a child develop a sense of belonging. Have the whole family participate in choosing photos and other family treasures to include in a collection that is displayed or accessible to every member of the family.

Collection Formats

Collection formats might include the following:

- *Framed hanging collection.* Hang an assortment of family photos in a hallway, guest bedroom, or other area with sufficient wall space (or take it to the ceiling when you run out of wall).
- *Catalogued photo albums.* Use matching or similar-size albums with good spines for bookshelf labels (see special notes on albums below).
- *Glass-covered table tops.* Place photos on a table top and then cover the photos with a piece of glass or Plexiglas cut to fit the table's dimensions.
- *Decoupage displays.* Decoupage panels are a wonderful way to memorialize photos from a special family occasion such as a fiftieth anniversary or first birthday.
- *Display in cabinets.* Set aside a glass-paneled cabinet for display of family photos or memorabilia.

Use Your Imagination

The family art gallery need not be limited to photos. Adding other cherished family possessions can enhance it. For example, a shadowbox of a baby's baptism might include a photo and also the infant's baptismal gown.

Here are some other ideas:

- Craft or art projects from several generations can be clustered together, perhaps in a series of pillows on a sofa. Needlepoint canvases and cross-stitched tea towels or hankies can be turned into pillows. Ceramic knickknacks, watercolors, and other drawings by family members of all ages can be framed and hung on the same wall. A child's crayon drawing can take on museum proportions when mounted and beautifully framed.

- Charm bracelets, old pocket watches, and other jewelry can be displayed in shadowboxes or deep frames.
- Eyeglasses—especially old wire frames—worn by various family members can be clustered together in a shadowbox.
- Old letters, certificates, diplomas, and even mortgages can be framed and hung together.
- Pieces of fabric and lace from old wedding gowns and other clothing may be used as background for mounting other unusual objects.
- Single pieces of china, figurines, silver spoons, or other implements can be collected to reflect a family heritage of collecting or using similar items.

About Your Photographs

Today many people have family photographs that date from the turn of the century. Caring for these photographs is much the same as caring for photographs that are taken today. To help preserve your family treasures—no matter how you decide to display them—observe these tips:[1]

- Always mat photographs before framing them. This holds them slightly away from the glass and prevents sticking. Old prints as well as daguerreotypes, ambrotypes, and tintypes that are bowed or warped will be difficult to frame because they must not be forced flat. Consider shadow boxes or other ways of displaying these photographs.
- When mounting a print, do not paste the entire print onto the backboard. Never use rubber cement or pressure sensitive tape.

- Aluminum frames are safe, lightweight, relatively inexpensive, and come in all sizes and colors. Wood frames can attract insects and give off gases that are harmful to the photograph.
- Display photographs in the lowest practical light level. Sunlight and fluorescent light will cause fading or discoloration. Special Plexiglas (UF-3) will filter out most of the ultraviolet rays. Dust, particularly dust formed by oil or gas heat, is harmful to photographs.
- When dusting framed photographs, use a dry untreated cloth. Do not use any cleaning solutions.
- Hang photographs on an inside wall away from fireplaces or heating units. Light, heat, and humidity present the greatest danger to the life of a photograph.

If you decide on storing prints in an album or box, here are some practical suggestions:

- Store black-and-white prints separately from color prints. Color prints are unstable and will not last as long as black-and-white prints.
- Unfortunately, the most popular methods of storing photographs (magnetic-paged albums, black-paper albums, and scrapbooks) will harm the photographs. It is better, and also less expensive, to store prints loose and flat in a box made of acid-free cardboard, chemically inert plastic, or steel with a baked enamel finish. Never keep a photograph that has begun to deteriorate in a box with photographs that are in good condition.
- Polyvinyl photograph sleeves are not wise for long-term storage. Look for polyester, polyethylene, or polypropylene pages that install in ring binders.
- Keep the prints in a cool, dark, and dry place where the temperature and humidity level will not fluctuate.

Creating Heritage

The family art gallery is likely to become an ever-expanding collection that becomes treasured by family members as years pass. Perhaps the greatest heritage it will foster is the sense of belonging it brings to your children, grandchildren and, possibly, many generations to come.

Build Family Character

9

I have a dream that my four children will one day live in a nation where they will not be judged by the color of their skin, but by the content of their character.

—MARTIN LUTHER KING JR.

A HIGH SCHOOL PRINCIPAL is reported to have said, "Too many of today's children have straight teeth and crooked morals." Character is the single most important ingredient of a strong family. Character is knowing right from wrong and acting responsibly—it is parents modeling integrity through honesty, courage, and unselfishness. Families exemplify character by the way they live—by involvement in the school and community, standing up for what is right, and serving others.

Start at the Very Beginning

Lessons of character are learned at home. Whether the values learned are negative or positive, the home is the child's most influential classroom.

Since most children spend the majority of their time at home during their first five years, the family is the primary place where values are learned. In *Teaching Your Children Values,* Linda and Richard Eyre observe that parents often make the mistake of becoming general contractors for their children—jobbing out important lessons in values to be taught by school teachers, athletic coaches, scout leaders, and religious leaders.[1] These subcontractors play an important part in shaping a child's character, but the job of character education is primarily the parents' responsibility.

Character Curriculum

Example is the best teacher when it comes to character formation. Character lessons are more easily *caught* than taught. In other words, children learn more from what they see than from what they hear. Think ahead and be intentional about your behavior. If you want your child to have good work habits, then *demonstrate* good work habits. If you want your child to be considerate of others, show that same consideration to your child, your spouse, and others.

To be most effective, Mom and Dad should agree on what values they want their children to learn, and then be deliberate about teaching them. Respect, integrity, hard work, honesty, morality, dependability, civic duty—these should make your personal list of the most important values to reinforce. Articulate and discuss those ideals with your children, and help them to learn what those values mean in terms of self-discipline and commitment.

Encourage your child to identify her own values, naming what is most important and listing her priorities. Then discuss how to live out those values in practical ways. Your child will learn to stand for her convictions in the midst of pressure if you have already engaged in family discussions, scenarios, or role-playing about the values you hold to be important.

You Are Your Child's Best Teacher

Life in general, and the home in particular, is a classroom in itself. Most of the best learning experiences happen in the routines of the day—and often at the most inopportune moments! By thinking ahead you will be prepared to make the most of the moment. For example, when you check out at the grocery counter and receive the wrong change, how do you handle the situation? Do you let the cashier know a mistake was made, even if it was in your favor? Do you pocket any extra change? What you do in the presence of your child will be what your child does in the future.

When a child has done something wrong and has the courage to tell you, praise him for being honest and then help him work out the consequences. Let the child know he is expected to take responsibility for his mistake. Then give support and encouragement as your child follows through to right the wrong.

Help a child who has made a bad decision by giving him or her a second chance. Then coach your child toward a better decision. Living out the consequences of bad decisions is often punishment enough.

Listen to the news with your child, read the same books, and watch some of the same television programs. This practice gives ample material for discussions on character! Identify and discuss character flaws that resulted in dire consequences for a tragic character. Point out the difference between the value that is displayed and the value you hope your child will embody.

Everyday Heroes

On the positive side, discuss the stories of everyday heroes. They may be people you know in your church or neighborhood, see on the local news, or read about in the headlines of catastrophic events, such as the attacks on the World Trade Center and the Pentagon. In most cases, stories of heroism are linked to good values and strong moral character.

10 Show Affection to One Another

No matter what you've done for yourself or for humanity, if you can't look back on having given love and attention to your own family, what have you really accomplished?

—LEE IACOCCA

D R. BRUCE PERRY, Chief of Psychiatry at the Texas Children's Hospital, has made an astonishing claim about family affection. Pointing out the value of hugs and kisses in raising healthy kids, he said, "Research shows that stroking and holding young children stimulates the brain by releasing hormones that are essential to growth."[1]

Commenting on Perry's research, psychologist and family therapist Paul Faulkner said, "Receiving loving touches and hugs from parents is as essential as receiving vitamins and calories!"[2]

Express Love in Many Ways

Parental and familial love is the number one ingredient for raising emotionally healthy children. Many parents assume their children are fully confident of their unconditional love, but that love needs to be communicated over and over again. You can send the message of unconditional love to your child by giving him or her your time, attention, respect, admiration, and affection.

Time to Love

It's been said that love is spelled T-I-M-E. Spending time with your child communicates love. Children love attention—especially the attention of their parents. If they don't get it, they will do whatever it takes to get it, even if that means destructive behavior.

Here are some ways to use time in communicating love to your child:

- Talk with your child. Don't limit your communication to homework or giving the dog a bath or asking how the ball game turned out. Talk to your child about his or her concerns and feelings. Is he facing any fears or worries? How does she feel about herself? Be open about your own feelings, and your child will feel safer sharing his feelings with you.

- Listen to your child. Be sure your child knows you are paying attention and that you consider his or her opinions to be important.

- Find ways to show you are proud of your child, not just for achievements and accomplishments but because of who he or she is. Let your child overhear you share your enjoyment and pride in them with others. Carry your child's picture in your wallet and display framed photos in prominent places in your home.

SHOW AFFECTION TO ONE ANOTHER

Like and Love

Let your child know you *like* him, as well as love him. Liking someone has to do with enjoying them for who they are—their personality, tastes, sense of humor, quirks, and idiosyncrasies. You may not like specific hairstyles or lipstick colors, but find something you sincerely do like, and let your child know it!

Respect

Respect from a parent instills children with confidence. Here are some suggestions for showing your children you respect them:

• Show confidence in your child's opinions by involving her in family decisions. Let her share some of the decision making about vacations, use of discretionary funds, or places to eat. Your child will have a greater sense of ownership and take more responsibility for outcomes.

• Consult your child for advice on a decision you are facing—a work situation, a decorating issue, or a choice of activities. Being an adult doesn't mean having all the answers. At the same time, don't burden your child with your problems. A major decision regarding your personal life is often a burden too heavy for a child to carry. Asking for your child's input is not the same as relying on his or her answers for direction.

• Within practical limitations, indulge your child's fantasy as much as possible. Let her know you take her dreams and goals seriously. Perhaps her dream is a trip to a theater performance in a big city. Try to fulfill that dream if you can.

• Introduce your child to your friends and other adults and let her participate in adult conversation. Include her in the discussion; don't just let her eavesdrop. Take your child to work with you and introduce him to coworkers and colleagues. He will know you are proud of him and come to appreciate the challenges of your career and work.

Be Available

Be sure your child knows she can get in touch with you at any moment and that you are available no matter what situation you are in, even if it is a business meeting, golf game, or movie outing. Make your family a priority and your children will likely do the same.

Apologize When an Apology Is Warranted

If you make a mistake or unintentionally say or do something hurtful, apologize for it. Ask for forgiveness and discuss what happened. When your child sees how you handle your mistakes, he will learn how to handle his mistakes.

Express Appreciation and Affection

Show appreciation to your child for keeping his room neat and clean, for not leaving the car with an empty gas tank, or for faithfulness in doing household chores. Give special thanks when he performs those tasks voluntarily!

Last, but not least, be affectionate. Share hugs before your child leaves home in the morning to go to school and have a big welcome hug when he or she returns. With your hugs and affection, you let your children know they have all the love they need right at home. Hugs and kisses should always be in ample supply. Sometimes the best way to get a hug from a child is to tell him that *you* need one, and only the special hug your child gives will do.

Be creative and fun in showing love to your spouse and children. You want your children to know beyond a doubt that they are loved!

11. Make Family Memories

One of the ironies of our fast-paced culture is that it calls for more leisure time to offset ever-increasing pressures, while at the same time it reduces the amount of time available to us.

—Dolores Curran

ONE OF THE GREATEST LEGACIES parents can give their children is happy memories. Happy childhoods don't end when we become adults. Those early experiences are an investment in our adulthood and make us who we are today.

Think back on your own childhood and some of your favorite memories. What made them happy? Good? Meaningful? Your most cherished memories may not be of the biggest days or grandest experiences of your life. What often makes a favorite memory is not the event itself but the person or persons with whom you shared it. Family memories are made from experiences shared with those you love the most!

In *The Writing Life,* Annie Dillard said, "How we spend our days is, of course, how we spend our lives." If our days are a rush and a blur, our lives will be a rush and a blur. One way to slow the rapid passing of time is to fit some out-of-the-ordinary activities into your schedule.

Obviously, family memories are made from doing things as a family. It doesn't matter *what* you do, as long as you do it *together.* Pursue a hobby, sport, volunteer activity, or recreation. Decide together what activity to share as a family. Then learn it, do it, and enjoy it together. In other words, make a family memory!

What activity seems most suitable for your family? Outdoor activities such as boating, camping, or hiking? Sports such as skiing, biking, or golfing? How about a family chess or Scrabble tournament? Is your family musically inclined? Then sing together, attend concerts, and learn to play new musical instruments.

Camping is one activity that seems to work for nearly everyone in most families—and it can be done in many comfort levels. Extended backpacking trips, RV trips, a week-long tenting and fishing getaway, and a cabin in the woods are all variations on the camping theme. Before committing to a camping trip, consider spending a night outdoors in your own backyard to see how your children adapt to the dark and to night sounds.

Once you feel your family is ready to brave the great outdoors, make an exhaustive list of everything you will need. Consult a web site or library for information on camping gear and double-check that you have packed all the needed supplies. When you are in the wilderness, it's a long trek home to get the ax or cook stove.

At the campsite, make it a family challenge to put up the

tent. While one person clears the sticks and stones off the tent site, another reads the setup instructions. Equip others with hammers to drive in the tent stakes. Your Scout-trained knot expert can put his or her skills to use to secure the tent.

Plan your meals ahead and divide up chores between the cook crew and the cleanup crew, and rotate responsibilities. Have backup meal plans in case the fish aren't biting. Assign another child the responsibility for having the first aid kit available, and another one to look after the fishing gear. Chopping the firewood and building a fire are activities that should be supervised by someone with experience. Teach each child campfire safety—how to build a fire and how to put one out completely.

Camping offers interests for all: hiking, swimming, exploring, maybe even rock climbing and rappelling. Once you get some experience, you will look back and laugh at your earlier missteps.

Cherished family memories are more likely made around a campfire than around the television. Build lives and make memories at the same time.

Celebrate Holidays in New Ways

Decide as a family that you are going to celebrate a traditional holiday in an untraditional way. Here are several ideas that other families have enjoyed:

- Wait until Christmas Eve to put up the Christmas tree, and spend the days before Christmas making ornaments and baking cookies—taking some of those ornaments and cookies to people who are homebound.

- Set aside the afternoon of Mother's Day to plant annuals in your flower beds. Give every person in the family a chore and make it a fun event. Serve homemade lemonade and have your first cookout of the summer to celebrate a garden full of flowers. One family that made this a tradition for years continued to plant flowers in memory of their mother at a local park.

- Have a no-frills, quiet evening at home on New Year's Eve. Enjoy sitting by a fireplace or watching a sunset together, reflecting on the year that has passed and sharing hopes for the coming year.
- Make family birthdays a time when the birthday boy or girl gets to decide the dinner menu and sit at the head of the table. Consider serving dinner using the best family china, silver, and crystal.

Load the Memory with Love

One family decided to make its own holiday. They called it "Fifty Hugs on Friday the Fifth." Every time Friday fell on the fifth day of a month, they celebrated by giving each member of the family fifty hugs. With two parents and three children, that meant a lot of hugs were shared in a twenty-four-hour period!

Every holiday and every occasion can become a memory if it's laced with an extra dose of love. The words of Mother Teresa are good to keep in mind: "I think the world today is upside down, and it is suffering so much, because there is so very little love in the homes and in family life. We have no time for our children, we have no time for each other; there is no time to enjoy each other."

12 Create Keepsake Boxes

For where your treasure is, there your heart will be also.

—Jesus of Nazareth

LONG AGO, when young women worked on their dowries, they filled their hope chests with various items for their wedding or new home. Many of their treasures were handmade and reflected the ethnic or national origin of their families.

Today, when the average marrying age is in the mid-twenties and goods of every kind are plentiful, young women and men are far less concerned about storing away items to furnish a home. Yet some version of a hope chest is still made by many furniture manufacturers. These days hope chests tend to be filled with items from the past. Nearly everyone has treasures that represent cherished memories they want to protect and preserve.

While some items may be displayed, others may be too delicate or personal to leave in the open. Placing them in a chest or memory box has several advantages:

- It is easier to share them with a special relative or friend.
- Special items all together in one place can be moved quickly in case of fire or other emergency.
- A well-constructed box can afford old or delicate items the special protection they need.
- The box and its contents will become a treasured family heirloom.

Memory Boxes for Your Children

At a very early age children begin collecting things of special importance to them. They seem to have a natural proclivity for finding and protecting personal treasures. Many baby boomers will admit to having their childhood cigar box—the traditional treasure box of post-WWII kids—in their attic.

Children can also learn to appreciate the personal treasures of their classmates and relatives. A peek inside another person's memory box helps a child understand what is important to the owner.

Before deciding to purchase or make a memory box, create one for yourself. Begin by identifying several items for inclusion, and take into consideration their size and preservation needs before deciding how to proceed. If you have a hope chest—or plan to purchase one—consider also creating a smaller box for small items to be placed in the chest. Once your memory box is complete, share it with your children. Let them know three things:

- why each item is important to you,
- that the items belong to you alone and your children may examine them only if you open the box, and
- that the children may have a special box of their own if they so desire.

Don't worry about encouraging children who show little interest in their own memory boxes. Some children are not quite mature enough to see any point in collecting. Others have already identified another receptacle for their treasures. Don't be surprised if the uninterested child has a change of heart later.

There are many memory box kits available in craft stores, through catalogs, and on the internet if you want to make each child's box yourself. There are also many attractive boxes available in mall stores and gift shops that can be personalized with brass nameplates or photographs. Even so, a homemade memory box often becomes a treasure itself when children grow up. Consider setting aside an afternoon to help your children make their own memory boxes.

Since children's boxes usually won't be used to store old or delicate items, you may opt to use containers that you already have and purchase a few inexpensive items for construction and decoration. Give your children the chance to be creative and make an object that is theirs alone. You might make one box yourself to give them inspiration, and then work with them as they create their own boxes.

Help Children Create Their Own Memory Boxes

Here are several suggestions for helping your child create his own memory box:

- Cover an empty shoebox inside and out in a collage manner, using images cut from magazines. Glue the pieces so the photos overlap and are of unusual shapes and sizes. Let them dry, and then coat the entire box with several thin layers of clear glue, allowing each to dry completely between coats to create a true decoupage treasure.

- Cover an old hatbox with fabric, gluing it on with watered-down white glue. Decorate the edges with bits of leftover braided trim.

- Cover a large cookie tin or popcorn tin with a solid color of craft paint. Allow children to paint their own pictures on the sides and lid, and spray the finished masterpiece with shellac after the paint is dry.
- For older children, use craft store wooden boxes as a base and hot glue beads, leftover lace, and other trims to the exterior. Attach fabric lining on the inside using hot glue.
- Purchase an inexpensive frame the size of your child's favorite photo. Glue the framed picture to the top of a hinged wooden box deep enough to stand on end to display the photo. Be sure the lid will remain securely closed when on display. Small magnets or Velcro tabs may be helpful.

Collecting

You will probably have little trouble deciding what goes into your box, but your children may need help. Remember that a child's memory box is *not* his baby book. Items from the first few years of a child's life are often a parent's treasures until the child is an adult. Kids may already have a treasure box containing pretty marbles or shells picked up at the beach. Explain that each memory box is different because the only things that belong there are things that have special meaning to the owner—the objects should be things he would never give away. Always let children add and remove items from their boxes as they grow. Let the boxes be theirs alone. Don't give children under ten years old family heirlooms or other items that are especially valuable or irreplaceable.

Finally, no matter how crudely constructed or trivial the contents of a child's memory box may seem, remember that they still belong to your son or daughter—even if that child is an adult and no longer living in the same house as his or her box. Make sure the box is given to them and not tossed out.

13. Take Family Vacations

A vacation frequently means that the family goes away for a rest, accompanied by a mother who sees that the others get it.

—Marcelene Cox

HEALTHY FAMILIES spend leisure time together. Dolores Curran, in her research on traits of a healthy family, identified three characteristics pertaining to family time together: The healthy family has a sense of play and humor, a balance of interaction among members, and shares leisure time.[1]

However, Roper polls of families with children between the ages of eight and seventeen indicate that the number of families taking vacation together fell from 53 percent to 38 percent in the last quarter of the twentieth century.[2]

Everyone Benefits

Families bond while taking vacations by getting away from the phone, television, and computer; devoting time to one another; sharing new experiences; and discovering new places. No matter where you go, traveling together is an adventure in itself!

Traveling to new places naturally broadens a child's outlook and increases his or her independence. Exploring new cultures and unfamiliar surroundings helps young people become more confident in handling new situations. It also develops a sense of curiosity about the world outside their community.

Parents experience many benefits from taking family vacations. Besides meeting their needs for relaxation and refreshment, a good vacation is rejuvenating and invigorating. Many parents find vacation time to be a good opportunity for reconnecting with their children's dreams, hopes, fears, ideas, and opinions.

Vacation fun is not limited to the week or two of actual travel time. The time spent planning and anticipating the vacation and then returning with souvenirs, watching home videos, putting photos in scrapbooks, and recalling stories also contributes to the overall vacation experience.

Don't Bust the Budget

Besides lack of time, one of the biggest reasons for not taking a family vacation is lack of money. The American Automobile Association's annual vacation survey shows that a family of two adults and two children can expect to pay an average of $223 per day for food and lodging.[2] Limited funds do not mean limited fun! With some creative planning, you can plan a fun vacation without busting the budget.

Every vacation doesn't have to be a dream vacation, but if a family desires a "trip of a lifetime," they can make it a family goal and work together to save money for it. Then enjoy the splurge.

Don't put off vacations until the funds are there for the fantasy trip. With careful budgeting and planning families can enjoy *some* vacation time together every year. Include vacation costs in the family budget, so the money is available to make it happen.

Like the once-popular Christmas Club plans sponsored by banks, open a separate vacation account to set aside money for trips. A painless way to save money is to keep a jar in the kitchen and periodically empty coins from pockets and wallets. Within a year you will have a lot of extra dollars to spend on vacation. One woman emptied her coin purse of all quarters every Saturday. She worked as a waitress and received a number of quarters in her tips. She discovered that over the course of a year, she nearly always had enough money for one plane ticket to a vacation destination point—and sometimes enough for two tickets!

Spending fewer dollars on vacation does not translate into a low return on the fun. In fact, spontaneous vacations can be less stressful and every bit as enjoyable as planned trips.

Planning Ahead Saves Money

Travel industry professionals agree that advance planning is one of the biggest factors for saving on travel costs. If possible, book reservations as much as a year in advance to get the best rates. Unfortunately, family vacations are usually taken during peak holiday or school vacation seasons when prices increase.

Once a budget is determined you can begin to narrow down your destination options. Vacation at the beach? A tour of a major city? A cruise on a family-friendly ship? Most major theme parks are surrounded by dozens of recreational options. A week at an all-inclusive resort also simplifies vacation planning—just be sure the resort offers something for everyone in the family.

Transportation is a high-cost travel expense. A long car trip halfway across the country may not be the most economical if you can find an airfare travel discount and make early reservations.

Accommodations are also a big-ticket expense in the vacation budget. Ask for family rates and any travel discounts, such as AAA, that can reduce costs. Be flexible about where you stay. A hotel two blocks from the beach instead of right on the ocean can save important dollars.

The internet offers unlimited possibilities to shop around for travel bargains, and online reservations often offer the best price. Online travel research is almost a hobby in itself! Airfares, car rentals, travel packages, accommodations, family-friendly destinations—it's all there.

14 Support and Comfort Each Other

A friend should bear his friend's infirmities.

—WILLIAM SHAKESPEARE

WHAT DO YOU DO WHEN TRAGEDY STRIKES? What do you say in these situations?
- Your child's friend or pet dies
- Your husband loses his job
- Your best friend's relative is sent to prison
- Your father is diagnosed with Alzheimer's disease

Death, divorce, or any kind of loss can cause life-changing grief. The desire to comfort family or friends during difficult times makes many people feel awkward and uncomfortable. They fear saying the wrong thing or being insensitive while trying to cheer up the one in difficulty. More than anything, they don't want to deepen the pain. As a result, they often withdraw from the relationship until life begins to return to normal.

Being a comfort to another person in times of trouble does not require special skills. Just remember these general guidelines:

- Recognize that it's not your job to solve the problem or impart pearls of wisdom. "I'm sorry," or "What can I do to help?" are often all you need to say.
- Listen. Really listen. Your quiet presence and undivided attention provide more comfort than you may realize. Be sensitive to what the grieving person is telling you about his or her readiness to share the grief—not everyone needs to talk it out.
- Stay in touch. Make contact every so often to say, "Just checking in," or "How are things going?"

Knowing the Stages of Grief

Psychologists have recognized some specific stages in the grieving process, although not everyone goes through every stage. Being aware of these stages can help the grieving and those who are trying to give comfort.

1. *Denial and shock.* The initial response is often disbelief that the event has happened.

2. *Anger.* During this stage the most common question asked is, "Why me?" Sometimes anger over the unfairness of death or loss may be projected onto others. Be patient during this phase. It will pass.

3. *Bargaining.* Many people try to bargain with God, often offering to give up an enjoyable part of their lives in exchange for the return of health, a job, or the lost person.

4. *Guilt.* People often experience guilt over things that were done or left undone prior to the loss. Forgiving oneself and accepting one's own humanity help resolve the guilt.

5. *Depression.* An overwhelming sense of loss may be accompanied by mood swings. Feelings of isolation and with-

drawal may follow. Encouragement and reassurance may not be very helpful to the bereaved in this stage.

6. *Loneliness.* Despite reentering the social world, the grieving person may still feel an acute sense of separation.

7. *Acceptance.* Acceptance does not mean happiness but rather that the reality of the situation is now fully accepted.

8. *Hope.* In this stage, the pain lessens and the individual begins to look to the future in a positive way.

People find comfort and regain control of their lives in many different ways. Each person is unique in his or her response. What works for one may not work for another. Grief is often compounded when family members are sharing a common tragedy. Adult family members have the added responsibility of trying to help children cope with their feelings of grief and loss while dealing with their own. The way the parent copes with loss and sorrow will definitely have an impact on the child's ability to deal with his or her pain.

Children often experience their first major loss when a pet or beloved older relative dies. Sometimes children grieve over events in which they were not directly involved, such as the shootings at Columbine High School in Colorado, or the terrorist attacks of September 11th. Parents should be sensitive to kids who have suddenly found that their world is not as safe or secure as they once believed.

Helping Your Child through a Tragedy

The National Education Association, among others, has published a series of guidelines for helping children through both personal and shared tragedies. Here are some strategies for helping children cope with the grieving process:

- *Rebuild and reaffirm.* Love and care in the family is a primary need. Spend extra time with children to let them know someone will take care of them. If parents are survivors, it is important to assure kids that their parents have reassumed their former roles as protectors and nurturers. Physical closeness is a must.

- *Talk it out.* Address the irrationality and suddenness of disaster. Children should be allowed to vent their feelings, and they need to have those feelings validated. Psychologists advise allowing kids to reenact the tragedy if they want to do so. Parents should be prepared for children to talk sporadically about the event, spending small segments of time concentrating on particular aspects of the tragedy. Since children are often reluctant to initiate conversations about trauma, it may be helpful to ask them what they think other children felt or thought about the event.
- *Write and draw.* Provide children with a special time to paint, draw, or write about the event. Adults or older children may help preschool children reenact the event, since they may not be able to imagine alternative endings—for example, if the car had just stopped . . . if the fire hadn't started . . . if the storm hadn't come onshore. Children need to understand that not every situation that begins as the disaster began will end in the same fashion.
- *Allow anger to be expressed.* Be prepared to deal with aggressive behaviors and accept the manifestation of anger, especially in the early phases after the tragedy. Encourage your child to punch a pillow rather than a person!
- *Express the facts.* Children want as much factual information as possible and should be allowed to discuss their own theories about what happened in order to begin to master the trauma or assert control over their environment.
- *Express hope.* Reaffirming the future and talking in hopeful terms about future events can help a child rebuild trust

and faith in his own future and the world. Parental despair often interferes with a child's ability to recover.

- *Allow for grief.* Issues of death should be addressed thoroughly. The child is not to blame for death. Furthermore, death is not a rejection of the child. Death is permanent and sad. The grieving process should be acknowledged and shared.

15 Establish Boundaries

A parent must never lose sight of the fact that the parent is filling a leadership role. The parent is the authority within the home because the parent bears the responsibility for the child's actions.

—Dr. William Mitchell

A PARENT'S JOB is to set the rules for the children. You must make certain they know what is expected of them and have an understanding of why certain behavior is required. A reason may encourage a child to obey a rule.

Clear Lines of Authority

Establish clear lines of authority in your family so everyone knows the chain of command when it's time to make decisions, resolve differences of opinion, or settle disputes. The chain of command in your family is likely to be related to your religious values and beliefs. In some cases, it is related to specific situations or issues—especially if one parent is assigned an overseas tour of military duty or is away from home for extended periods. Make sure your children know to whom they should turn for a definitive decision regarding their behavior and activities.

Your child should obey immediately, exactly, and without question. In some cases, immediate obedience can mean the difference between life and death. Precise and wholehearted obedience does not mean that you have the right as a parent to become a dictator, but rather that you have a responsibility to help your child learn the importance of following instructions willingly and accurately—a lesson that reaps benefits in all of life.

Obedience without question means your child responds to you without requiring an explanation. Certainly a child should be free to question the reason for a directive after he has obeyed it, but he should not be allowed to withhold obedience until you have given him a satisfactory answer. In requiring unquestioned obedience you are preparing your child for the reality that he or she will always be under someone's authority.

Respect for You

Insist that your child speak and act toward you with courtesy and politeness. Do not allow your child to speak to you with rudeness, cynicism, sarcasm, or disregard, and forbid the use of crude or vulgar language. If children are allowed to show disrespect in the home, they are going to display even worse behavior toward other adults. Specifically, they will disrespect those who are in authority over them, such as teachers and principals, law-enforcement officials, worship leaders, and all other authorities. Teach your children that even though they may not agree with everything you say and do, they are still under your authority as long as you have material, financial, and legal responsibility for them.

Also teach your child to respect your possessions and those of their siblings. Your child should be taught to knock before opening a closed door, respect your privacy in a bathroom or bedroom, and stay out of your closets, purse, wallet, or other personal possessions without expressed permission from you.

Recognize that your child does not need to know all the details about your past life. Share with your child what you believe is helpful, but never make your child your confessor or confidant.

Manners and Courtesies

Teach your child the common courtesies of polite society:
- Open doors for others.
- Say "Please" and "Thank you."
- Express thanks verbally and in writing.
- Take turns.
- Listen closely when others are speaking.
- Help seat others at a table.
- Escort or help others who are in need of physical assistance.

Also teach your child good table manners—to use various utensils appropriately, eat with a closed mouth, and maintain good posture at a dining table. A child with good manners will be welcomed in virtually all settings and by all people, regardless of social or economic differences. As one parent said, "My child may not grow up to be the richest or best educated child or highest-ranking person in a room, but my child will have impeccable manners, and because of that, my child will always be acceptable and welcomed, regardless of his race, color, ethnic background, or any other factor related to his life!"

Limitations and Schedules

Parents have a responsibility for setting boundaries that define and regulate virtually every aspect of a child's life.

- Establish a consistent bedtime and awakening time. Children on a regular schedule tend to arise alert and sleep soundly and peacefully.
- Set a time for meals. Regular meals help keep a child's energy level constant throughout the day.
- Set a time for doing homework.
- Make a list of chores for the child to do daily or weekly.
- Establish rules regarding school attendance and completing homework.
- Set limits regarding time with friends and boundaries as to where a child may go.
- Regulate what your child takes into his or her life, including what he or she reads, sees, experiences, and ingests.

Rules should be clearly stated so children know exactly what is expected of them. Rewards for obedience and consequences for failing to obey should be clearly spelled out up front. A child should be able to repeat a family rule and know the context in which the rule applies, and also be able to recite the consequences for disobedience.

Recognize that rules are always applied to context. "Be quiet" is an appropriate rule for a worship service or a visit to the library. It is not, however, a rule that applies to attendance at a football game.

"Don't ask" is a good rule to have when shopping at a supermarket, especially if it means "Don't ask me to buy you a toy or treat." It's not a rule, however, that should apply to school. In a school context, children should be encouraged to ask pertinent questions!

Maintain consistency in establishing and enforcing rules. What you require of one child, require of other children in the family (with allowances, of course, for an older child to have a slightly later bedtime or other privileges than a younger child). Rules should be adjusted for age and maturity, and can be relaxed or tightened according to a child's track record of obedience and responsibility.

In his book, *The Christian Family*, Larry Christensen writes about a housewife who said to him, "I had the meanest mother in the world. While other kids ate candy for breakfast, I had to have cereal, eggs, or toast. . . . My mother insisted upon knowing where we were at all times. . . . She had to know who our friends were and what we were doing. She insisted if we said we'd be gone an hour, that we be gone one hour or less. . . . We had to wear clean clothes and take a bath. . . . We had to be in bed by nine each night and up at eight the next morning. . . . She always insisted upon our telling the truth, the whole truth and nothing but the truth, even if it killed us—and it nearly did. . . . I thank God He gave me the meanest mother in the world."[1]

Clearly Defined Roles for Others

Set clear boundaries for the involvement of in-laws, stepparents, and any other adults who have regular interaction with your family (such as babysitters, nannies, or housekeepers). You don't need to give elaborate explanations about your rules and choices—as parents, you have authority over your children and over all who abide in or visit your home.

16 Confront Tough Issues

Train up a child in the way he should go—and walk there yourself once in a while.

—Josh Billings

NO FAMILY IS IMMUNE to life's hard situations. No matter how well a family has its act together, the most perplexing issues have a way of coming right in the front door. The most important message you can give your child is to let him or her know that you practice an open door policy—your child can talk with you anytime, anywhere, about anything. In fact, children need to learn that their parents are the preferred providers of answers to difficult questions and information about tough issues.

Children don't have to go out of their way to be confronted with hard issues. Some of them are aired on the nightly news and appear in banner type across the front page of the morning newspaper. School shootings, terrorist attacks, and the violent aspects of war come daily into our homes and make children feel frightened and insecure.

Be There!

Watch the news or read the newspaper together and discuss the events with your children. Sharing your own perspective and feelings with them helps create a safe and open climate for dialogue. Don't wait for the perfect moment to bring up hard issues. Use the moments that occur in your everyday routine to talk about drugs, sex, guns, the possibilities of war, and terrorism.

Ask your child how he or she feels when hearing the news, and then discuss your own feelings—disappointment about the failures of peace initiatives, fears over terrorism and school shootings, sadness at hearing about teen suicides and alcohol-related deaths. Respond to tragic events, and don't shrug them off with an air of helplessness. Talk it through with your children to help them see they are not helpless victims. Help your children sort out right from wrong about what is happening in the world.

Children's Fears

Beyond the violence in the world, children are confronted with the recurrent issues of drugs, sex, and alcohol. A national survey of parents and kids released last year by Nickelodeon and Talking with Kids (an ongoing campaign of the Kaiser Family Foundation and Children Now) showed that half of the eight- to eleven-year-old children surveyed said violence and discrimination are big problems for kids their age; 44 percent said alcohol and drugs are big problems; and 33 percent of ten- to eleven-year-olds indicated that pressure to have sex is a concern.

Family experts concluded that parents need to "talk early and often with their kids—before adolescence—when kids are most receptive to hearing from them."[1] Once children reach their teen years, they turn to sources outside their home to learn about the facts of life.

Ten Tips for Talking with Your Kids

Parents need to earn the right to be heard. At times, "Because I said so" has to serve as a parent's final answer, but as a child grows older parents need to give their children opportunity to discuss both sides of an issue. Begin talking with your children when they are young so the more difficult and sensitive issues will be easier to deal with as they grow older.

The Talking with Kids campaign offers ten techniques for communicating effectively with your children:[2]

1. Start early. While your child is young, talk, talk, talk to one another. Never stop. Be sure you are the one to talk about the tough topics first. Begin those discussions while your child is still preadolescent.

2. Initiate conversations. Don't wait for your child to approach you with hard questions—they may never feel comfortable enough to do that. Take the initiative.

3. Talk about sex and sexuality. Even though you may find the subject of sex awkward to bring up, you can be confident that your eight-year-old child is hearing about it somewhere. When your children learn about sex, you want them to hear about it from the perspective of your values.

4. Invite open discussion, but don't embarrass or criticize your children when they express their ideas or opinions.

5. Communicate your own values. Research shows children want and need moral guidance from their moms and dads. In discussions on sex, drugs, and alcohol, let them know clearly what your values and opinions are.

6. Listen to your child. Paying close attention to your child

will give you opportunities to introduce valuable discussions on sensitive issues.

7. Be honest. You don't need to tell everything when your child obviously isn't ready to hear the full explanation, but make sure everything you choose to say is true. Being honest earns your child's trust.

8. Be patient. A difficult conversation can take time. Give your child the time he or she needs to ask hard questions and get satisfying answers.

9. Use everyday opportunities to talk. Bring up sensitive topics as part of your day—when you hear them in the news or read about them in the newspaper.

10. Talk about it again. Most discussions about challenging topics are too much for a child to absorb in one conversation. Bring it up repeatedly and ask the child what he or she is thinking about the whole matter.

Strong families make good communication—about everything—a top priority.

17 Be Forgiving

Never does the human soul appear so strong and noble as when it forgoes revenge and dares to forgive an injury.

—E. H. CHAPIN

AT THE CORE of any healthy family is the ability to forgive freely, frequently, and fully. All members of a family need to know that when they err—inadvertently or even willfully—they can confess what they've done, express sorrow over their misdeeds, and ask for and *receive* forgiveness.

Make sure every person in your family fully understands what forgiveness is and isn't. Forgiveness is *not* a denial that injury or harm has been inflicted. Forgiveness is *not* saying, "It didn't happen. It didn't hurt. It didn't matter." Neither is forgiveness saying, "Let's just move forward and forget about it."

Forgiveness *is* saying, "You hurt me, but rather than hold onto that hurt I choose to release it from my heart." Forgiveness says, "I do not like what you did, but I continue to love you and value our relationship."

All children need to know that no matter what they do—and no matter what consequences they must pay as part of a disciplinary process—their parents still love and value them.

Forgiveness and Justice

Forgiveness and justice go hand in hand. Make sure boundaries and rules are in place so your child knows what you consider to be acceptable and unacceptable behavior. One family adopted this threefold criteria for deeds that needed to be punished:

- Hurting another person physically or seeking to hurt another person emotionally
- Destroying or damaging another person's property
- Willfully hurting your own self physically or engaging in behavior that will bring about emotional or spiritual harm

Each of these areas was further defined by the parents according to their specific beliefs and values. The mother noted, "Our children knew, even before we knew, when they had done something that warranted punishment. I can count on one hand the number of times they asked, 'What did I do to deserve punishment?' The good side was that they also knew that once they had paid the 'price' of punishment, they would be fully restored to the family as a beloved child and sibling, without any residual resentment or bitterness. Sometimes our children asked for their punishment to be immediate, so they could get back to being fully restored to the family."

Justice requires consequences for misdeeds. Punishment has three purposes:

- To make a hurtful person learn from his or her mistakes
- To help a person who is wronged feel a sense of equilibrium
- To help the person who has hurt someone feel that tangible penance has been made

Punishment, of course, can range from requiring a public or private apology, payment for damages done, withdrawal of a privilege, or time alone to contemplate one's misdeeds. Again, forgiveness is not saying, "All can be swept under the rug." Rather, it is saying, "I will not diminish my love for you on the basis of what you have done."

Any time you exact a form of punishment, discipline, or justice for a wrong committed against you or another person, make sure the punishment is concrete, the person who has erred can pay the price without further personal injury to himself, and that the victim of the crime knows that a punishment has been required. Once a punishment is fulfilled, move forward—don't revisit old errors, and don't hold onto an unforgiving attitude.

Avoid a Cycle of Revenge

In his book *Experiencing Forgiveness*, Dr. Charles Stanley identifies a twelve-part cycle of forgiveness:[1]

1. We feel wronged.

2. We have difficulty in dealing with our hurt. (The hurt lingers.)

3. We try to take a detour away from the hurt. (We seek to flee.)

4. We deny the pain. (We try to outrun or outlive it.)

5. We dig a hole for the pain. (We repress our hurt feelings.)

6. We feel defeated. (We develop bitterness and resentment.)

7. We experience defilement. (Our pain stains or taints our relationships with others—we have a shorter temper and less compassion.)

8. We become discouraged about life. (We lose our inner peace.)

9. We become desperate. (We long for the peace we've lost.)

10. We engage in destructive behavior—against others or even against ourselves. (It is at this point that an unforgiving spirit can readily cause an addiction or a violent outburst.)

11. We begin to deal with the root cause of our pain for what it is—a state of unforgiveness. (We recognize we must forgive even if another person has not sought forgiveness or confessed error.)

12. We experience deliverance from pain as we forgive.

The process, of course, can be greatly shortened if we will immediately move toward forgiveness when we are hurt, rather than allowing hurt to linger. At times this means directly confronting the one who has wronged us and saying, "I choose to forgive you. You have hurt me but I will not carry any burden of hurt in my heart." At other times, forgiveness means asking God to free you from the hurt you feel by saying, "God, I feel hurt. Please heal my wounded heart of all feelings of rejection, alienation, sorrow, and loss. I trust you to deal with this person who has hurt me in a way that brings about your justice—I release them fully from my hand and place them in yours."

Quick to Seek Forgiveness

Just as we must be quick to offer forgiveness to those who have hurt us, we must be quick to seek forgiveness when we have wronged others. No misdeed is too small to seek forgiveness. It takes courage to ask someone to forgive you. So muster up your courage!

Don't allow hatred, revenge, or bitterness to seep into your spirit. You will be the worse for harboring those emotions, which can fester within you for years. If allowed to go unchecked and unhealed, the emotions of hatred, revenge, and bitterness can destroy your ability to have peaceful, open, transparent, trusting relationships with others.

Forgiveness Produces Freedom

Forgiveness creates an environment in which a person can truly feel free to manifest love, joy, peace, patience, kindness, and gentleness. Forgiveness is the ultimate antidote for chronic frustration, impatience, anger, jealousy, bitterness, agitation, and inner turmoil. If you are often upset, burdened, out of control, or uptight, ask yourself, "Is there someone I need to forgive? Do I need to ask forgiveness of someone?"

Forgiveness unshackles us from old hurts and frees us to fully become the best we can be. Complete forgiveness is required if we are ever to reach our personal potential and experience lives marked by meaning, purpose, and satisfaction.

18 Teach Your Children about Family Heritage

If you don't know [your family's] history, then you don't know anything. You are a leaf that doesn't know it is part of a tree.

—MICHAEL CRICHTON

WHAT DO PEOPLE HAVE in common with trees, carrots, teeth, and hair? Roots! A root, according to Webster's dictionary, "functions as an organ of absorption, aeration, and food storage or as a means of anchorage and support."

Roots for humans are ancestors and heritage. Like plant roots, our family roots provide nurture and support. We did not drop into this planet out of the blue. We are connected to generations that have gone before us.

Pass on the Family Heritage

Exploring our root system, or family heritage, teaches us a lot about ourselves. Sharing that heritage with our children enlarges their perspective about who they are. For instance, discovering that there is a long line of teachers and educators in the family can encourage a child's natural bent toward teaching and education. Searching the family tree for any roots of inherited musical talents may reveal another Brahms or Beethoven.

Hopefully you have been the recipient of your family traditions and stories—the oral or written history of your ancestry. If so, you have a responsibility to pass on that heritage to your children. Queen Mary once said to one of her relatives, "You are a member of the British royal family. We are never tired, and we all love hospitals." Even today the royal family makes many public appearances and raises funds for charities.

History is not a subject that naturally appeals to many children. Be creative in making family history come alive for your kids. Alex Haley's book and TV miniseries *Roots* popularized the search for family heritage. Genealogy clubs, web sites, newsletters, and celebrations of ethnic festivals and holidays are enjoying a revived interest.

Ethnic Foods

Food is a big component of a cultural heritage. Typical Americans are a blend of nationalities that immigrated to the United States over the centuries. Introduce your children to their family heritage by enjoying foods from the nations of their family origin.

Mexican and the Americanized Tex-Mex foods are popular to persons of all heritages. In recent years, salsa sales surpassed ketchup sales in the United States! That tells us a lot about changing American tastes and demographics.

Chinese, Japanese, Vietnamese, Thai, Korean, and East Indian restaurants offer a tasty way to sample a wide array of

Asian fare. Middle Eastern falafels, shish kabobs, and tabouli; Greek baklava; and Polish sausage can be found in many regions. Italian food—lasagna, pizza, spaghetti—has become such an American standard that many no longer label it ethnic food.

Some ethnic foods are eaten on certain days celebrating a national heritage, such as Saint Patrick's Day with a dinner of corned beef and cabbage, a typical Irish meal. The Jewish holiday Hanukkah Feast of Lights features potato latkes, applesauce, and suphganeyotm—a jelly-filled yeast doughnut.

African American foods are a part of the Southern cooking tradition of greens, okra, barbecued ribs, corn bread, and hoppin' John. Native American community dinners feature wild onions and fry bread.

Heritage Quilt

A family quilt makes a cherished heirloom to pass on to your children. Design quilt squares around themes of your national heritage—a national flag or flower, a national landmark, symbols of immigration such as a Viking ship or the Ellis Island entry point, an outline map of the country of origin. With embroidery or indelible ink, record the dates of immigration and the names of your ancestors.

Make your quilt a project for the extended family. Invite a number of family members, young and old, to contribute a square. When you receive all the squares, sew them together to make a large quilt for display. If you don't sew, inquire at a local fabric shop about a local quilter. Take pictures of the quilt, and enlarge the photos so each child can have a representation of the family heritage.

Read History

Study the history of your ancestors' native lands to learn more about their lives and possible reasons why they immigrated to the United States. Even if you don't know the specifics of their lives, you can get a general understanding of what daily life was like at the time in history in which they lived. Novels of historical fiction also give a glimpse of life in the "old country."

19 Rediscover Old Family Traditions

Family traditions counter alienation and confusion. They help us define who we are; they provide something steady, reliable and safe in a confusing world.

—SUSAN LIEBERMAN

WEBSTER'S DICTIONARY says tradition is "the handing down of information, beliefs, and customs by word of mouth or by example from one generation to another without written instruction." Traditions are something you do and talk about naturally as a family.

Establishing family traditions creates lasting memories for your children. Traditions are an important part of what holds people together as a family or nation. We all have rituals that touch our hearts. From the contents of the picnic basket on Memorial Day to the sharing of gifts during the holiday season, each family has its own special ways to celebrate.

Time spent with our families helps us develop a keen awareness of ourselves within the family framework. Your current family life is no doubt similar to and different from that of your parents and grandparents. Similarly, the adult lives of today's children will both resemble ours and be brand new. Traditions are a bridge creating a strong, meaningful link between our present lives and what we hope for our children and grandchildren.

As a parent, you may want to revive long-held family traditions or create new ones. You may come up with a special bedtime ritual for your child, go to the same lake house every summer, go apple picking every fall, or tell stories on New Year's Day. You may decide that your family should have a special time to read together, have an end-of-day chat over hot chocolate, or start a board game tournament that continues week to week. *What* you do is never as important as doing it together.

If you're inspired but feel overwhelmed at the thought of starting or enriching your family's traditions, take it slowly. Elaborate plans that require lots of preparation are unnecessary. Remember that the goal is not to have lots and lots of traditions, but to have meaningful ones. Start by choosing just one tradition and have the family think of ways to make it satisfying and meaningful.

You may want to select a particular category of traditions—birthdays or holidays, for instance—or you may decide to start a tradition that's missing. Would your family life improve if you had a different kind of nightly dinner? Can you find a new way to express your love for your children in a bedtime tradition? Is it time for a family reunion that brings generations together?

Rediscovering Old Family Traditions

Find family joys from the past and share them with your children. Choose a time when the family is together. Ask your spouse about the traditions his or her family enjoyed and share some of your own. Kids will naturally ask questions and express opinions. You might also have this conversation with grandparents present. Talk about forgotten traditions and discuss whether any of them should be revived in your own family.

Even though resurrected traditions may be new to some family members, there are ways to quickly adopt these times as part of the family identity. Here are some tips:

- Find out if there are special rituals or objects such as candles, books, or clothing, that were always a part of the tradition and try to use them, or replicas of them, in your reclaimed tradition.
- Invite extended family members who were part of the original tradition to join your family on these occasions and encourage them to share their memories.
- Take pictures, and begin a scrapbook or album dedicated to remembering traditions.
- Keep a diary of events and participants in traditions that are annual or occasional.
- Make sure every family member has a role to play in the tradition. Children should not only enjoy the time together but also feel that they have played an important part in carrying it forward.

Establishing New Traditions

The phrase "new traditions" sounds like an oxymoron, but they often develop when a family has an experience together that everyone wants to repeat or remember. A common element usually exists that helps establish the tradition. It may be a place, person, object, piece of clothing, special event, or simply the way things are done. Common threads give the event continuity while providing flexibility in keeping the tradition year after year.

Traditions should never be used to place guilt on any member of the family. In fact, a tradition should always be viewed as an opportunity to change and expand your family's togetherness around a common theme. When kids decide they don't want to participate, here are a few things you might do:

- Ask why they don't want to participate and what they don't enjoy about the event.
- Allow them to bow out if they really want to.
- Tell them the rest of the family will miss them and they're welcome to change their minds at any time.
- Find ways to accommodate whatever concerns they express when you ask why they don't want to participate. For instance, a common family tradition is to be home for the holidays. Often the togetherness is focused on a particular meal or event at the core family's home. As the family gets older and scatters, some have found they can preserve the important "together" aspect of the holiday tradition by changing the venue to a ski resort, beach, or other nontraditional spot.

New traditions do not necessarily have to involve *every* family member *each* time. One family has a tradition of celebrating the thirteenth birthday of each child with a special four-day, "Mom-or-Dad-and-me" trip. The child chooses which destination and parent she wants to accompany her. No other family members tag along and the parent and child have a great experience together to launch the teen years.

When establishing a new tradition, decide *why* the tradition is important to your family and concentrate on keeping that aspect of the tradition as the constant element.

Finally, be sure to explain to younger children especially why a tradition is important to your family and how it makes your family unique and special.

20 Establish New Holiday Traditions

I once wanted to become an atheist, but I gave up—they have no holidays.

—HENNY YOUNGMAN

HOLIDAYS ARE EVENTS that occur annually in celebration or memory of an event or person. Some holidays, such as Thanksgiving, Christmas, and Hanukkah, are widely celebrated, and signs of these special occasions can be seen for weeks before the actual day.

Many people struggle through holidays because of a painful personal event that took place during that time in the past, or because of the recent death of a loved one. For others, unhappy childhood memories have marred their ability to enjoy a special holiday with their families. People who have moved far away from home may also find it difficult to enjoy holidays because of feelings of loneliness or cultural differences.

For these people, the joy and celebration going on around them often deepens their depression. Tragically, these attitudes are usually passed on to other members of the family—especially children—in one measure or another.

Out with the Old, In with the New

Most holiday blues sufferers sincerely desire to enjoy the holidays. Establishing *new* holiday traditions may be the most effective way for them to ease old associations and feelings.

New traditions are important when establishing a new family—especially a blended family where members may have different expectations. Sometimes the best reason to begin a new holiday tradition is simply because no one in the family can identify an object or activity that really says, "*Now* it's the holiday!"

Suggestions for New Traditions

Here are some suggestions for finding and establishing your family's own set of new holiday traditions:

- If you have a sad association with a particular holiday, purposefully schedule the next big, joyful event on or near that date. Get married, host a reunion, or have a baby baptized or dedicated. Try to involve new people who were not a part of the past tragedy. Celebrate this new event annually along with or in place of the holiday.

- Involve your family and close friends in helping assemble a new assortment of decorations for major holidays. For example, you might develop a mini flag collection for the Fourth of July (or Veterans Day) or a tabletop village (instead of the traditional tree and ornaments) for a winter holiday.

- Plan a family volunteer project. Help serve Thanksgiving dinner at a local shelter, collect blankets and coats to distribute to the homeless, or help deliver meals and supplies to homebound seniors.

- Many cities have outdoor picnic concerts during warmer months. Get the whole family involved in selecting a different theme for each year's picnic feast. Prepare food that fits the theme.
- If your family is theatrically or musically inclined, prepare a show to share in local nursing homes. Invite friends to join you.
- Take a family trip to a special destination.
- Decorate the front door or yard of your house in a holiday theme. Place a particular holiday-related object on the table during family meals.
- "Adopt" new family members for the holidays. Consider inviting an elderly acquaintance, a child from a nearby orphanage, or a college student unable to go home for the holiday. Invite a friend who has lost a loved one to become a member of your holiday family.
- Bake or cook holiday food as a family and package extra portions in special containers to give as gifts or party favors. Find a special recipe that your family loves and spend a whole day making enough to share with friends. Let non-cooks assemble packaging and create personalized labels ("Jones' Family Favorite Fritters" or "The Smiths' Special Herb Mixture").
- Enter a walkathon or marathon together. Many families have a loved one who suffers or has died from a disease like cancer or AIDS. For these families, participating in research fund-raising events together is empowering and comforting. Finish the day with a party, meal, or a toast to the person in whose honor your family participated. Take time to share special thoughts about the person.
- Plant a garden together or visit a local produce farm to gather vegetables or fruit to turn into preserves. Treat yourselves to a special celebration dinner at the end of the day.

(You might fix such a dinner in a slow cooker in the morning, or go out.)

- Start a collection of homemade decorations. Choose a unique medium or collection of materials each year. For example, one year use Styrofoam balls, glue, and beads. The next, make ornaments from dough or clay and bake them. Another year, make mini picture frames to hang on the tree. Each family member's contribution will be unique and treasured for years to come.
- Volunteer as a family to be Salvation Army bell ringers.
- Attend a holiday parade and take an elderly or disabled neighbor with you. Or create a family float for a public participation parade.

Regardless of the activity, the purpose of a tradition is the special unity that comes when family members work to make a celebration special, joyful, and meaningful.

21 Balance In-Law Tension at Holidays and Every Day

When first faced with the reality that the family you married into does things differently, the warmth of tradition can take on a chill.

—Marge Kennedy

IF IT WAS A PERFECT WORLD, all young couples contemplating marriage would have the "in-law talk" right after they had the "kids—yes or no" discussion. But in this less-than-perfect world, most people marry without giving serious thought to how the dynamics of in-law relationships will affect their marriage and family.

Ideally, when new members are added to a family through marriage, the parents embrace the new son- or daughter-in-law as their own, and vice versa. In most relationships, however, this bond is not automatic, but rather the product of years of mutual give and take among family members.

The holidays can add land mines to the in-law battlefield, even when a truce or cease-fire has already been negotiated. First, there is the problem of where or with whom the holidays will be spent. Then, you have the conflict of differing traditions. Throw in long trips, last-minute shopping, cooking, cleaning, whiny kids, and social obligations, and the scene is set for instant explosions at the first sign of in-law conflict. Sadly, many families in conflict will point to events during a holiday as the time when a major break in a relationship occurred.

With some planning and a few key ideas gleaned from family counselors and psychologists, you can make your time with in-laws as enjoyable as possible.

The Basic Principle for In-Law Peace

The first and foremost principle of in-law peace is for all parties to recognize the core family unit. When a new family is established through marriage, the newly married couple owes their first allegiance to each other. If or when children join the family, that allegiance is extended to include them. This primary allegiance must be kept in mind when hard choices present themselves.

As much as possible, couples should talk about their unity in the face of in-law conflicts *before* they occur. If sides must be taken, stick with your spouse. Voice your disagreements in private, out of earshot of the rest of the family. Couple unity is the critical foundation for successfully working out the rough spots in an in-law relationship.

With that basic principle as a basis, below are a few other ideas to help reduce your anxiety about in-law relationships and the issues that arise around the holidays.

Advice for Daughters- and Sons-in-Law

- If you already have a tense relationship, don't wear your feelings on your sleeve. Don't assume that everything your in-law says is aimed at you or meant as criticism. If you feel verbally attacked, try not to respond with anything more than "Hmm," or in a quiet, steady voice say, "I'm not going to discuss that right now. Let's focus on making this a great holiday for the rest of the family." If that doesn't work, leave the room temporarily. Come back smiling.

- Set visiting time limits in advance. If you are the host, call the in-laws ahead of time and tell them you're looking forward to having them as your guests for very specific dates. If you are the visiting family, let the in-laws know exactly when you plan to arrive and leave, and ask if that schedule fits their plans. In either case, make definite plans for the day before and following the visit.

- If you are the host, provide the best accommodations you can for your in-laws. However, unless there is some compelling reason to do so, it's generally a bad idea for couples to relinquish their own bedroom just because it's larger or nicer than other accommodations. Take obvious extra care to prepare the visitor's sleeping area with things that will make your in-laws feel at home. Extra pillows, an empty drawer, a place to open suitcases, and a small bouquet of fresh flowers all say, "We're glad you're here."

- Spend moments alone with a parent-in-law talking about his or her life. For example, ask your mother-in-law about her first holiday dinner as a wife. Listen for clues about her relationship with her own mother-in-law and ask questions. After your conversation, thank her for sharing and let her know you appreciate her life experiences and value her as a person.

- Don't let yourself be dragged into a family quarrel that doesn't involve your husband or children.
- Allow your in-laws to spoil your children a little during the holidays. Let kids and grandparents all know that exceptions are being made only because of the special celebration. Make sure grandparents know about dietary or other restrictions affecting your children's health.
- If tension arises, concentrate on lowering the volume of your voice even when others raise theirs. They are likely to take your cue. Do your best to keep a negative situation from escalating into an all-out feud.

Regardless of how difficult it may be, you'll never be sorry if you treat your parents-in-law with dignity and respect.

Advice for Mothers- and Fathers-in-Law

- Don't assume your in-law is trying to take your place or drive a wedge between you and your son or daughter. Even if that is true, the ultimate responsibility for your relationship lies with your child. Conversely, be cautious about assuming that a new daughter- or son-in-law will warm to you in a parental role—now or ever. Many in-law relationships grow into special friendships. You can be supportive and still allow your in-law child to take the lead in developing a relationship with you.
- Your son or daughter's home is not an extension of your own. Respect the new home and couple as though they were your new neighbors. Don't expect their home to be like yours. As for things you need—don't go looking for them in drawers and closets. Take the basics you need with you when you visit.
- Don't bring unexpected contributions to the celebration dinner. Ask in advance what you may contribute. Offer

to help with cooking and cleanup chores, but respond graciously if your offers are rejected.

- Allow your son- or daughter-in-law to make some mistakes without judging or offering hindsight advice. Instead, share some of your own early goofs. It will make you more approachable, and they'll be more likely to ask your advice in the future.
- Be realistic about how much time you can spend together. Remember that your family has expanded, as have your adult child's responsibilities. Try to remember how these new relationships affected you in the early years of your marriage.
- Make sure you clear gifts or goodies for the grandchildren with their parents first. Don't be offended if they nix the idea for a specific gift. Ask for suggestions for a replacement.

Regardless of how difficult it may be, you'll never be sorry if you treat your son- or daughter-in-law with dignity and respect.

Many people develop wonderful, mutually satisfying relationships with their in-laws. With a little self-control and true understanding, nearly every in-law relationship can attain peaceful coexistence. And remember, people change as they age. A relationship that has been tense for twenty years can still blossom into genuine warmth and affection.

22 Research Your Family Tree Together

People will not look forward to posterity who never look backward to their ancestors.

—Edmund Burke

MAPPING OUT A FAMILY TREE can be a great opportunity for younger children to learn more about where they come from and how they are related to people they have never met. Researching your ancestors is also an opportunity for your family to contact lost relatives, interview older relatives about ancestors, and reconnect with your extended family as they join the search for your mutual heritage.

Beginning a family tree isn't as difficult as it may sound, but be prepared to get very involved in the process. Most people start out thinking they'll just gather basic demographic data—name, birth and death dates, and names of spouses and children. Soon, however, they are also interested in occupations, burial places, immigration information, physical characteristics, and other aspects of an ancestor's life. Before you begin set aside a folder where you can toss incidental bits of information.

Five Basic Steps

Genealogical research, like any other kind of research, involves five basic steps:

1. *What do I already know?* Most people can name two or three generations of ancestors. Assemble all the information you possess about your relatives and organize it in written form. If you plan to keep your records on your computer, be sure to back them up on a disk or CD and print out a new hard copy whenever you have made several revisions. Now is also a good time to create a blank tree template on which to begin your family record. Expect the tree to sprout new branches as you uncover new relatives. Next, interview relatives to help fill in the information gaps and reveal relatives you'd forgotten or didn't know about. Ask for access to diaries, records, and letters. Ask about family rumors and scandals. Document everything you learn.

2. *What specific question needs to be answered?* You will need to focus on a few individuals at a time (usually several closely related members of the same family), and also focus on just a few questions about those individuals. There is an unlimited number of questions that one could ask about each ancestor:
   - Name?
   - Place of birth?
   - When, where, and whom did they marry?
   - Number, names, and sex of children?
   - Where did they live?
   - Occupation?

- Religious, military, or school affiliations?
- Physical characteristics?
- When, where, and how did they die, and where are they buried?

For each individual, make a research plan document. List the questions you want to answer on the left, and on the right list steps to take to obtain the answers.

3. *What sources of information should I use?* There are two basic types of information sources: primary and secondary. Primary sources are those that were created at or near the time of an event, usually by someone who was a direct observer or participant in the event. Secondary sources are those that were created either much later than the time of the event or by someone who was reading or interpreting a primary source. Primary sources are preferable to secondary sources because they are more likely to be accurate, but secondary sources may lead to primary sources.

If you don't have many good primary sources such as birth, death, or marriage certificates, you may benefit from research that has already been done by others. While it is possible that this research may contain errors, it may save you a great deal of time in locating the primary sources you need. You will find many of these resources on the internet.

Other sources can be purchased on CD-ROM and then searched on your own home computer. Information on obtaining records from America's states, counties, and towns is available through a number of channels. (Refer to the book *Ancestry's Red Book* edited by Alice Eichholz.) Many sources, especially census records, can be searched at your local public library or Family History Center (FHC). Public libraries also often have city directories or copies of old local newspapers. Family History Centers are usually listed in the telephone book under "Church of Jesus Christ of Latter-Day Saints" and are operated by the Mormons for the benefit of all genealogists.

4. *What do these resources actually tell me?* In your search be careful not to miss information using too narrow a time period or overlooking a misspelled name. Keep a log of the sources you use so you don't retrace your steps.

5. *What are my conclusions?* Occasionally you may find conflicting bits of information. These conflicts do not necessarily mean you're on the wrong track, just that there are errors in the records. Use additional sources to verify the fact and document your sources for future reference. Then decide whether or not you are ready to place that person on the tree.

You don't need to spend a lot of money to begin your research. You only need access to the internet and some time. Internet access is free at most public libraries.

23 Get Involved in Politics that Impact the Family

Every word and deed of a parent is a fiber woven into the character of a child that ultimately determines how that child fits into the fabric of society.

—DAVID WILKERSON

THERE ARE NUMEROUS WAYS for a family to become involved in politics, and the result of involvement is the same—the more individuals and families are involved in political decisions and processes, the stronger a democracy becomes!

Model Values

Parents inevitably model these basics of life:

- *Respect for those in authority.* Always voice respect for elected officials, even if you do not share their opinions.

City, county, and state officials should be respected as much as national officials. In many cases, *local* political decisions have greater impact on your immediate daily living than *national* decisions. Local politics affect the schools your children attend, the roads on which you drive, and the safety provided by local fire and police departments.

- *The function of government.* Let your children know that you favor the orderly transition of power, civic involvement in politics, the established legal system, and that you support change if it is for the good of *all* citizens, not just a fraction of the society. Show your child that you respect minority rights, even as you adhere to majority rule. Show your child how to protest in ways that are legal, civil, rational, and persistent.
- *Personal freedom and liberty.* Your child will learn various definitions in school but will associate values with those terms based largely upon what you say as a parent. Let your child know how you feel and what you think about terms and phrases such as democracy, freedom, dictatorship, liberty and justice for all, equality before the law, the right to pursue happiness, and rights vs. privileges.

Discuss Political Issues in Your Family

Use the dinner table or long car trips as an opportunity to discuss various political issues with your children. Let your children know what you believe about issues they are likely to confront in school discussions and classroom debates. Talk about laws and policies related to the following issues:

- Racial discrimination
- Sexual orientation
- Abortion and alternative approaches to abortion
- First Amendment rights (speech, association, religion)—including separation of church and state and prayer in schools

- Second Amendment rights (right to bear arms)—gun control
- The balancing of individual rights and national security

When discussing these issues it is essential that you follow some basic guidelines:

- Avoid political labels. Speak to your children in terms of values and beliefs. Avoid labeling a person "republican" or "democrat" without giving your child good definitions about what those labels mean. The same goes for "conservative" and "liberal." Keep in mind that in other cultures, the values we associate with being liberal might be considered conservative, and vice versa!
- Give reasons for your opinions and cite facts that support them.

Model Positive Political Behavior

Parents can model positive political behavior to their children in a variety of ways. Consider doing some of the following:

- Take your children with you to the voting booth.
- Attend neighborhood caucus meetings. If it is not appropriate for your children to attend with you, discuss with them why you are going. Afterward tell them what happened at the caucus.
- Periodically attend city council and school board meetings. This is especially important if you feel strongly about an issue on the agenda. Let your opinion be heard.
- Show respect and honor when singing the national anthem. Stand up. Take off your hat as the national flag passes. Know the words to the Pledge of Allegiance and the "Star Spangled Banner," and speak or sing those words with pride.
- Pay your taxes. Whether you think taxes are fair or unfair, pay them! Let your child know that paying taxes is a part of responsible citizenship.

- Write to your local congressperson or senator—or even the president. Let them know your opinions regarding political decisions, pending legislation, and decisions related to foreign policy. Share your letter with your family. In some cases, you may want your family members to help you draft a letter and have all family members sign it.
- You may also want to consider writing letters to the editor of a local or national newspaper. Again, let your entire family know what you are saying and why.
- Consider volunteering for the political party of your choice. You can participate with contributions, by posting signs and bumper stickers, wearing buttons, or becoming involved in phone banks, door-to-door visits, and local or national rallies.

Stay Informed

In this rapidly changing political world, it is important to stay informed of decisions, big or small, that are being made in our nation and around the globe.

- Subscribe to one or more politically oriented magazines, newspapers, email services, or newsletters. Choose at least one form of input that is contrary to your political party or position—at minimum, you will be informed about what the other side is thinking and saying; at maximum, you will be given pause to evaluate and perhaps reevaluate your position on various issues.
- Have a copy of the Declaration of Independence and the Constitution of the United States (including the Bill of Rights and all amendments) in your home. You may also want to introduce your teenagers to the "Federalist Papers" and other writings of our Founding Fathers.
- Subscribe to a daily newspaper. Encourage your child to

read articles dealing with national and international issues.

Consider planning trips to your state capitol and Washington, D.C. As you visit various monuments and government buildings, remind your child that these are *their* monuments and offices as citizens of the United States. Express personal ownership and responsibility for the function of our democratic government.

24 Get Involved in Your Child's School

The school will teach children how to read, but the environment of the home must teach them what to read. The school can teach them how to think, but the home must teach them what to believe.

—CHARLES A. WELLS

FAR BEYOND ATTENDING an occasional school program or a parent-teacher conference, parents need to be involved regularly and routinely in their child's school. The family is ultimately the primary source of education for any child.

In *Strong Families, Strong Schools*, Secretary of Education Richard Riley cited a study done by Barton and Coley. This landmark study conducted in 1992 revealed that most of the differences in achievement observed across the states could be attributed to home practices more than school practices. Three specific factors were mentioned in the study: student absenteeism, the variety of reading materials available in the home, and excessive television watching. These factors accounted for nearly 90 percent of the differences in the average performance on standardized tests.

Require School Attendance

Parental involvement in a child's school begins by requiring that your child attend classes. Beyond mere attendance, it is important that you insist your child shows up at school academically prepared—in other words, with homework completed and a positive attitude toward school, learning, teachers, and principals.

As a parent, you set the tone for how your child approaches learning and the degree to which your child remains interested in learning, studying, and accomplishing academic goals.

Help with Study Skills

The family is the prime place for children to learn the following:

- *How to ask questions.* Encourage your child to be curious about the world around him or her—to ask how, when, what, and where questions.

- *How to categorize information across a variety of subject areas.* Help your child synthesize what is being taught at school with the practical world of the home and community. Point out examples of "theory in action" to your child as you shop, drive to and from school events, and discuss the day's local, national, and international news.

- *How to bridge old and new learning.* Keep your child learning and studying during the summer months, reinforcing what he or she has learned during the previous year.

It is in the context of the family that children best learn how to challenge themselves, take notes, analyze data, and prepare for tests. Do your best to help your child acquire these valuable lifelong learning skills.

Supervise Homework

Talk to your child about his or her homework. Never do your children's homework for them, but make yourself available to answer questions, offer assistance, and check over answers. In checking your child's homework, be alert to plagiarism. Insist that your child write his or her own themes, essays, and book reports.

One study conducted by the National Commission on Children showed that almost three-quarters of the students surveyed between the ages of ten and thirteen said they would like to talk to their parents more about schoolwork!

Supply Educational Materials in the Home

It is a parent's responsibility to determine how many and what types of books and other educational materials are available for a child to read. It costs nothing but a little time and interest for a parent to go with a child to the library on a weekly basis! The library is also a great source for magazines, videos, and audiotapes.

Parents who are able to afford a home computer or encyclopedia (either in CD-ROM or book form) give their child a valuable resource. At minimum, a parent should provide a child with a good dictionary and thesaurus.

Choose to give good books as birthday and holiday gifts—both fiction and nonfiction. Choose classics, as well as books about special interests your child may have. You might also want to purchase classic movies and performances of well-known plays as part of your video or DVD library.

Get to Know Your Child's Teacher

Discuss your child's educational progress with your child's teachers in an ongoing manner.

- Ask your child's teacher, coach, or bandleader for suggestions. They may be able to give you guidance about how to contribute to your child's success and socialization in school.
- If at all possible, both parents should attend parent-teacher conferences that are scheduled by the school. Ask questions. Get details about your child's performance. Ask how your child interacts with other children and participates in class discussions. Ask what values your child displays in the school setting. Ask what you might do to help improve his or her grades.
- Ask your child's teacher what values he or she is emphasizing to your child. Not all schools and teachers have values that reflect what you may be teaching at home. Knowing what values your child's teacher holds can help you mediate at home. You can reinforce or explain what a teacher is saying or provide thorough background to help your child withstand and even refute a set of values that are different than the values you hold. Teach your child how to refute others' values in a way that is respectful and nonconfrontational. If the value differences between your family and your child's teacher are extreme, you may want to request your child be transferred to another teacher's classroom.

If your child is in public school, you must recognize that certain religious concepts and truths will not be taught. At the same time, you can expect, and even require through consultation with a school principal, that your child not be required to study a religion or embrace religious practices other than your own, participate in value-related discussions that are contrary to the values you hold as a family, or role-play or participate in small-group scenarios that reflect behavior you consider to be immoral or unethical.

Attend School Events

Attend open house nights and school fairs. These events give you an opportunity to visit classrooms, see students' work on display, and talk to teachers and school specialists. Also attend your child's school athletic competitions and fine arts performances, art shows, speech contests, and concerts—even if your child is not a player or performer.

Your child will enjoy watching his or her classmates perform, and attending these events will help your child see that you are interested in all aspects of education. Attendance at such events may trigger an interest in your child to become involved in sports or fine arts programs. By all means, attend these events if your child is on the team (or bench) or in the cast (or working backstage).

Send a Message

Active involvement in a child's education sends the message that you value learning, hard work, dependability, and discipline in accomplishing tasks (including homework), and curiosity about the world at large. These are traits that build up a child's esteem and lay a foundation for personal success.

25 Help Your Child Prepare for Higher Education

I am still learning.

—MICHELANGELO

IT HAS BEEN SAID that the two most important decisions a person makes between the ages of fifteen and thirty are the choice of a spouse and the choice of a college. As a parent, be there to help your child make the wisest choice possible in each category. In the end, the choice of a college may have great impact on your child's choice of a spouse!

While your teenager may seek independence and have a can't-wait-to-get-out-on-my-own attitude, most teens are also fearful about making the leap to college. With independence comes many unknown factors and new responsibilities. Help your child grow into the college experience by becoming an active advocate for higher education long before he or she is ready for college.

Start Early

Even when your children are in elementary school, talk to them about higher education: "You'll be glad to know this when you go away to school some day." "That's something you'll enjoy doing in college." Statements like these should become a normal part of family conversation. Let your child know that you believe he or she is capable of pursuing higher education. Place value on getting as much education as possible.

When your child enters middle school or junior high, begin to drive by college campuses or trade schools as you travel through various cities. Give your child a familiarity with different types of schools—community college, college, university, Bible school or seminary, military school, or vocational school.

Aptitude Testing

One of the greatest gifts a parent can give a child is a good round of aptitude testing while the child is still in junior high or in the first two years of high school. Aptitudes are innate abilities—your child's giftedness or natural talents. Children who discover their natural gifts have built-in confidence that they will succeed in school and at work.[1]

Skill Development

Help your children turn aptitudes into skills. Encourage them to take lessons in areas of aptitude. This will give children added confidence and a head start on a career path.

Recognize that working on one skill can help your child develop related skills. Music training, for example, is of great benefit to virtually all children—even those who aren't naturally gifted musicians. Educational research has repeatedly shown that musical training is directly related to math and general organizational skills. Children who take music lessons and practice regularly also develop greater personal discipline and time-management skills.

Even if your child does not have large-muscle coordination aptitude, he or she can benefit from classes that encourage physical fitness, team play, and general physical coordination—dance, modeling, or drill-team activities. Such classes can help your child develop physically as well as mentally!

Academic Development

By all means, place high priority on homework. Reward children for exerting maximum effort, even if they don't earn top grades. Children don't know what they are capable of doing until they give their best effort to any task, including studying for tests, writing papers, and completing projects.

In holding out the future of higher education, you are giving your children an incentive to study hard and do their best in every area of academic pursuit.

If your child is lacking in essential areas—reading, basic math skills, or study skills—find a tutor who can help the child in these areas. They are vital for lifelong learning even if your child does not go on to higher education.

Encourage Your Child's Pursuit of Special Interests

Is your child fascinated with birds? Gardening? Cooking? A particular sport? Encourage your child to learn as much as possible about his or her area of interest, to practice skills associated with that area, and to meet people who are skilled and use their skills for the benefit of others. A child's interests tend to vary over the years, but the pursuit of each area of interest can provide a valuable incentive to read, research, consult experts, practice skills in a disciplined way, and benefit from conversations with mentors.

In showing an interest in the interests of your child, you send powerful messages: "You are valuable," "Your opinions and ideas count," and "You are capable."

College Familiarization

Early in high school, begin to send for college brochures. A wide variety of directories and publications are available to help your child discover schools that he or she might be interested in knowing more about. See Petersons.com for a list of helpful publications as well as suggested timetables for attending college nights, taking SAT and ACT tests, and filing paperwork.

During your child's sophomore and junior years of high school, begin visiting colleges. Your child may want to participate in a college weekend or supervised visit. Be sure to pick up a catalog of courses and degrees offered to make certain the school offers degree programs in your child's area of interest and aptitude.

Applications and Acceptances

Recognize that filing applications for college is going to be a part-time job for your child from the completion of the junior year of high school until mid-fall of the senior year. Help your child manage his or her schedule to allow sufficient time for completing applications, essays, and requests for recommendations.

Preparing for the Expense

Discuss with your child the costs associated with going to college. Beginning when your child is in junior high, insist that your child save a portion of any allowance or earnings. Should your child not attend college, the money saved will provide a valuable head start toward pursuing a career or living independently. Let your child become an active participant in paying for college tuition and fees. He or she will take the academic side of college a lot more seriously when helping to pay for it!

The Social Preparation

Even as you help your children prepare intellectually and financially for higher education, help them develop the social skills necessary for becoming responsible college students—help them learn how to get along with a roommate, take responsibility for eating correctly and sleeping sufficiently, budget time and money, and communicate in effective ways with peers and professors.

Preparation for Life

In becoming a strong advocate for higher education, you are preparing your child for responsible adulthood. You will be helping your child set, pursue, and achieve goals, as well as plan for his or her financial future. You will be guiding your child toward the maximum career success possible: the coupling of aptitudes, skills, and information.

The higher your child aims, with realistic preparation toward reaching goals, the greater the likelihood that your child will live a rewarding, satisfying life. Surveys continually show that those who attend institutions of higher education earn more money, lead more stable and responsible adult lives, experience greater health, and are better prepared for retirement.

26   Read Together

Literature gives us a memory of lives we did not lead.

—Mason Cooley

PARENTS, as their children's first and most important teachers, are uniquely qualified to pass on the richness of literacy. Unfortunately, too many parents are passing on the poverty of *illiteracy*. At a time when one in three American households owns a computer, more than 44 million adults in the United States are functionally illiterate, meaning that they do not have the reading, writing, speaking, or math skills necessary for everyday life. Illiteracy costs taxpayers $237 million per year in welfare payments, crime, remedial education, and poor job performance. The number of illiterate adults is growing each year by approximately 2.25 million people![1]

Parents, make sure your children don't add to that number! You can instill a love of books and information in children by reading aloud to them from a very early age. The ritual of the bedtime story is far more than an opportunity to help your child quiet down and get ready to sleep. There are many good reasons to read aloud:

- Reading exposes children to cultures and adventures they may not be able to experience.
- Reading increases a child's vocabulary and encourages independent reading.
- Reading helps children feel empathy and compassion while providing a parent and child the opportunity to spend more time together.
- Many educators believe that reading aloud increases listening ability and memorization skills and increases the chances that the child will be a lifelong reader. A child whose parents read aloud to her is more likely to read aloud to her children.

Research has shown that children who read *succeed*. Reading and education help break the cycle of poverty, crime, and hopelessness. Today's best-equipped schools and public libraries provide books, computers, and a wide range of programs to prepare young people to live and work in the twenty-first century.

Gear Reading to Your Child's Interests

Children are motivated to read if they can learn about things that interest them. Take time to find the right books to make reading an exciting activity for your child. Children's interests vary widely. Many children, especially boys, prefer nonfiction over fiction. They will call upon their reading skills to pursue an interest in snakes, racecars, trucks, or dinosaurs. Other children love to read about a recurring character or books in an adventure series.

Combining reading with fun activities is also a way to motivate children to read. A Baltimore teacher recently reported, "My students were overjoyed when they found books on how to make paper airplanes. They used every skill they had to break down the words that would help them learn to make the fastest airplane. They also started to look at reading differently when we used a book to learn how to make a great ice cream soda." These activities help children see a real purpose in improving reading skills.

The National Reading Research Center also found reading as a social activity to be very important. Researchers learned that visiting the library with family, reading aloud to family members, and trading things to read with friends helped make children into readers.

Reading Together

Parents can establish reading as a family activity very early in a child's life. Picking a particular time of day or location in the home to sit quietly and read conveys that reading is important to the family. Reading to one another as you travel in the car or listening to audio books is another effective way to engage children.

Set aside a quiet time each day to share books with your children when they aren't tired. Give them as much time as they need to look at the pictures before you begin reading. Follow your children's lead. Let them turn the pages and choose which pictures they want to view. Read the story dramatically, using animated facial expressions and expressive gestures. Allow them to ask questions, and ask your children what they think is happening in the story.

Reading can become an excellent experience for taking turns. For newer readers, read and pause so your child can fill in words. For example, ". . . and she saw a ___!" With a familiar story or a story told in pictures, you can read one page, and then your child can "read" the next one, and so on. This turn-taking style can continue as a family ritual as children grow.

Although the life of a parent is often hectic, you should try to read with your child at least once a day at a regularly scheduled time. Don't be discouraged if you skip a day or don't always keep to your schedule. Just read to your child as often as you possibly can.

If you have more than one child, spend some time reading alone with each child, especially if they're more than two years apart. It's also fine to read to children at different stages and ages simultaneously. Most children enjoy listening to many types of stories. When stories are complex, children can still get the idea and be encouraged to ask questions. When stories are easy or familiar, youngsters may even help in the reading.

Establishing a family reading night will enhance family communication while encouraging reading skills and a love of books. Choose a classic that the whole family can enjoy and read together. Each family member can take turns reading aloud to the others. Reading in this fashion turns the book into a serial adventure.

Taking the time to read with your children on a regular basis sends an important message: Reading is fun, worthwhile, and mind expanding!

27. Eat Together as Often as Possible

Home is the wallpaper above the bed, the family dinner table, the church bells in the morning, the bruised shins of the playground, the small fears that come with dusk, the streets and squares and monuments and shops that constitute one's first universe.

—Henry Anatole Grunwald

TRADITIONALLY, the family dinner table is a place of communion, fellowship, and a means of reconnecting with the people who are most important to us. It is a place to nurture relationships, exchange news of the day, and talk about the future. Memories are made at the dinner table. Someday your children will look back on family dinners with fondness, and you will look back wistfully, missing the chaos of trying to get everyone to the table while the meal was still hot!

Sadly, over the past fifteen or twenty years, eating together at the family dinner table has become an uncommon occurrence in many homes. Family members come and go from activities and obligations; parents work late and children have cyberfriends, homework, or television to keep them company. A recent Harvard Medical School study of 16,000 children found that about 17 percent of those studied ate dinner with their families "never" or "only on some days." Forty percent ate dinner with their families on most days, and 43 percent ate dinner with their families every day.[1]

Busy schedules are not the only problem. For many families, making the meals is also a big issue. In many homes working mothers regard meal preparation as dashing into a deli, picking up takeout, or ordering pizza.

Making family dinners a priority is not easy, but the long-term benefits are worth the effort. Research by the National Center on Addiction and Substance Abuse consistently shows that the more often children eat dinner with their parents, the less likely they are to smoke, drink, or use illicit drugs.

Sitting down at the table together is still one of the best ways for families to stay connected. The family dinner offers a natural forum that fosters togetherness. It can afford all family members a chance to share their lives and receive encouragement and support. Regular family meals also provide children with a much-needed safe haven of stability in a world that is often confusing and frightening.

Making Changes

Families sometimes face insurmountable barriers to eating dinners together regularly. If Mom works during the day and Dad works the evening shift, there may be only a couple days each week when eating dinner together is a possibility. Families with these circumstances have to be a bit more creative and flexible about their mealtimes. For instance, the family might plan to have breakfast together every morning. *Which* meals are shared is far less important than the process of sitting down together to talk and eat.

Here are a few tips to help your family get the most out of your mealtimes together:

- See that every member of the family has at least one task to accomplish in the meal preparation. For example, setting the table, putting the food on the table, preparing the salad or bread, or clearing the table after the meal.
- Don't feel guilty if family dinners are not a daily event. Start with what's possible at the moment and move toward the goal of eating together several times per week.
- The family dinner should be a relaxing, pleasurable occasion. Keep conversation upbeat. Unpleasant topics, negative criticism, and judgment are not appropriate dinner fare.
- Always involve your kids in the dinner discourse. Ask their opinions. Ask what their friends are saying about current events and topics of interest to parents and kids alike. Specific questions to children ("Who do you think should win this year's election?" "How many bites did you get on your line when you and Dad went fishing Saturday?") are more likely to trigger conversation than general questions ("How was your day?"). The art of conversing and learning how to take turns speaking are important social skills for school, home, and everyday life.
- Consider a fun dinnertime ritual. For example, pick a "word of the week." For the first meal of the week, one member of the family chooses a word from the dictionary to introduce to the rest of the family with its definition. Each member of the family must use the word once during the dinner conversation at each meal for the rest of the week. Each week, expose your family to a new word, and, potentially, to some

big laughs as family members sneak the word into their conversation. Remember always that laughter is the best dinnertime music.

- Turn off the TV and radio. Unplug the phone or turn off the ringer. Don't let interruptions disrupt this special time.
- Change the family dinner location occasionally. How about an afternoon picnic, dinner under the stars, or Saturday breakfast in your child's room?

Invite Ideas from Other Family Members

Do you wish your family could spend more time around the table together? Changing family eating patterns will take some forethought and cooperation from your family. It's a good idea to involve your children, especially teens, in the commitment to have more family meals. Next time the family is gathered around the table, ask these questions:

- Out of twenty-one possible meals each week, how many do we eat together on average?
- Are there any barriers to increasing the number of meals we eat together?
- What three things can we do to increase the number of meals we eat together?
- What are three positive things about eating meals together?

If family dinners are not a regular part of your household schedule, scheduling more meals together may initially be met with some resistance. In time, however, the pleasure and security they provide will have everyone looking forward to meeting at the table.

28. Visit Cities or Towns with Family Roots

Happiness is having a large, loving, caring, close-knit family in another city.

—GEORGE BURNS

THE SEARCH FOR HOME is a powerful emotional drive. Many adults who have grown up apart from their extended family of aunts, uncles, cousins, and grandparents are eager to learn about the people and places with whom they share natural bonds.

Making the journey to visit the places your ancestors lived helps fill in part of the puzzle. Ask who, what, when, where, and why questions. If some of your ancestors are still living in the area from which you emigrated or moved, now is the time to make the trip to meet them. They will no doubt be eager to meet you as well. Don't postpone this trip too long; the opportunity won't be there forever.

Local Resources

If you can't find any surviving relatives, you are on your own to explore the town or city and track down clues to family connections. A good first contact to make would be the local historical society. In small towns these are likely staffed by volunteers who will be eager to talk to you about their town in days past. An advance call or letter to set up an appointment will assure that you make a good contact.

If you can't find a telephone listing or address for an historical society, call the local library for assistance. A retired librarian who has lived and worked in the area for many years is often a great resource. Also call the town newspaper to find out where the archives of back issues are kept, and if they are available to the public.

An excellent source of official family information is the county courthouse where registers of births, deaths, and marriages are kept. These records are accessible to the general public.

Marriage and baptism records may point you to places of worship where family members were married. Visit the place of worship they attended or where they were baptized or married. You may even meet some people who knew them. Any names and dates you can get from baptism or marriage records will be helpful for putting together the big picture of your family background. Local cemeteries are another good source of family history. Sometimes you can gather interesting information from headstones and grave markers.

Another stop in your journey could be a visit to the senior center to meet and talk with some of the retired locals. Who knows? Such a visit could turn up someone who was a child when your relatives lived in that town.

Once you get started in discovering your family history, keep going down every possible path until you find the information you are looking for. And if you don't find any trace of your ancestors, visiting the city in which they lived will at least give you a sense of connection. Take photos to share with your family when you return home.

Visit the Nation of Your Ancestors

Another great experience for family history buffs is a visit to the "old country." You may not have any information about the specific town or city your ancestors came from, but a trip to their nation is a worthwhile experience. People who have made that pilgrimage have felt immediately at home and connected. They experienced a sense of belonging or level of understanding they did not have before.

While visiting the country you may be fortunate enough to acquire more details about where your ancestors lived so you can explore specific cities and villages, or find the family farm. You may be able to trace the steps they took if they left their native country and boarded a boat to America. Visiting that place can give you a renewed appreciation of the pioneer spirit and courage of your ancestors.

Even though your elementary-age or adolescent children may not have the slightest interest in meeting strangers, visiting small towns, or exploring cemeteries, keep a record of names and dates, and compile a book of pictures to pass on to them if and when they want to make those same family connections.

29 Take Special Care of the Elderly in Your Family

Sure I'm for helping the elderly. I'm going to be old myself someday.

—LILLIAN CARTER

THE STATISTICS ARE RATHER DRAMATIC—about one in every eight people in America (35 million individuals) is over sixty-five years old, and that number is expected to double in the next thirty years. The Administration on Aging also projects that the eighty-five-and-above population will increase from 4.2 million in 2000 to 8.9 million in 2030. America is rapidly getting older!

Traditionally, families have cared for their infants, children, and older adults. About 95 percent of all care for the elderly is unpaid, including care from families and informal caregiving arrangements. However, social changes—smaller families, more women in the workforce, and increased longevity of older adults—are affecting the ability of family caregivers to meet the needs of their elderly relatives.

The good news is that something is being done about the situation. More information is available, and more assisted living and long-term care facilities are being built to meet the demand.

Even with these positive developments, we must ask ourselves these questions: What are the needs of the elderly, and how can those needs be met in a caring and loving way?

Activity Level

The first step is to assess the activity level of the elderly relative. Is the person able to get safely in and out of the bathtub, drive safely during the day and night, cross a busy street without being confused, and use the stove without causing injury or damage? If you need help in assessment, contact a doctor or geriatric professional.

After assessing how much care your older relative needs, assess your own commitments to determine how much time you can devote to caregiving. Also contact other family members to determine their availability and willingness to help. With all parties involved, determine how much assistance you can give collectively and whether you need help from an outside caregiver.

Socialization

Old age can be isolating. As the body begins to slow down, the outside world seems to go faster, and the elderly tend to stay indoors. Isolation brings depression and a loss of self-esteem. As much as possible, engage the elderly in activities outside the home to help them stay connected. Senior centers, retired volunteer services, and foster grandparenting are just a few ways the elderly can remain engaged in outside activities.

Intergenerational activities are especially meaningful and invigorating to the elderly, and they enhance a sense of well-being. Civic and religious centers often provide a good setting for different age groups and events. Meeting for a meal at a local restaurant gives elderly people an opportunity to be out of the house as well as get together with other family members. Go to a restaurant where the noise level is low and there is easy access to the dining area.

Slowing Down

Aging also slows down some aspects of mental capacity. Confusion and memory loss are not unusual. This does not mean, however, that a person has Alzheimer's disease or dementia. Many elderly people are still able to solve complex problems, learn new skills, remember meaningful rituals, and accomplish mental tasks. Your goal as a caregiver should primarily be encouragement, provision of mental and social stimulation, and provision for safety and health needs.

Check with a doctor if you suspect confusion or mental problems beyond normal signs of aging. If a serious problem arises, you may need to engage a home healthcare or senior-service agency for extra help in attending to your relative in the home.

Be sure your loved one is getting some exercise if it is physically possible. Walking in the neighborhood or at the mall is a healthy activity. Encourage your elderly family member to walk with a partner in a safe area.

Loss of Independence

Most elderly people desire to stay independent as long as possible. As long as parents are healthy, they can remain in their own homes. When people age, however, they eventually lose their self-sufficiency. According to the Administration on Aging, the at-risk people are the 4.2 million Americans who are over eighty-five years of age; those living alone without a caregiver; older people with physical or mental impairments; and those who are abused, neglected, or exploited. The crucial questions are these:

- When should I intervene on behalf of my loved one's well-being?
- When is it time to consider alternate living arrangements—such as an assisted living center?

Do your research to find the best match for your loved one, and then visit various environments, returning several times to those you believe may be suitable. Look specifically for friendly staff members who are engaged in meaningful interaction with the residents, the cleanliness of the facility, pleasant mealtimes and dining facilities, and opportunities for planned group activities, social events, and opportunities for learning.

Making this transition is one of the most difficult times in your life and the life of your loved one. Consult with others who are facing or have faced similar circumstances.

Care of the elderly and the well-being of the caregiver are equally important considerations. Be sure you have your own support team as well!

30 Honor and Respect Elderly Members of Your Family

There was no respect for youth when I was young, and now that I am old, there is no respect for age—I missed it coming and going.

—J. B. Priestley

AGING IS HARD ENOUGH without the loss of dignity that often accompanies it. In his book *The Journey of Life: A Cultural History of Aging in America*, Thomas Cole points out that "improved medical and economic conditions for older people have been accompanied by cultural disenfranchisement—a loss of meaning and vital social roles."[1]

How a society treats its most vulnerable people—children and elderly, the ill and disabled—is an indication of the level of civility of that society. Once revered, today the elderly are often forgotten or ignored in a fast-paced, youth-dominated culture.

Luke Gormally, director of the Linacre Centre for Healthcare Ethics in London, England, proposes three reasons why the elderly are to be loved and respected:

1. The elderly need acceptance.
2. The elderly are our ancestors, and children should honor *all* their parents.
3. We need to relearn the value of human life.

The Greatest Gifts

How can we show love and respect to those who have loved and cared for us? For the elderly, time and attention are the greatest gifts—far more precious than any material possession.

Older people tend to be isolated and often feel forgotten. Keeping in touch with them lets them know they are remembered and cared for. If you don't live in the same town, telephone often, visit as much as possible, and write letters to keep them informed. They will feel included if you tell them about the regular happenings of your day, including your work and the activities and accomplishments of other family members. Many older people have email access to keep in touch with their grandchildren. Encourage the whole family to take turns writing to Grandma and Grandpa.

The Heritage of Family Stories

Encourage older people to share stories and memories from their past. The Navajo call their elders "walking libraries" because they keep the family informed of tribal history. It is their responsibility to pass down knowledge from previous generations.

One of the most meaningful ways to honor your older relatives and preserve family traditions is to record their stories in audio or written form. Even if some of the memories are painful (war, family disagreements, the loss of loved ones), talking about difficult stories as a family can help heal generational wounds. Encourage grandchildren to put their grandparents' words and pictures in scrapbooks or memory books to pass on to their own children.

Empathize with the elderly in their circumstances. How do they feel? How do they need help? How would you feel if you were in their situation? Pay attention to their worries and fears, and be an encouragement. Help them have a positive outlook on life. Ask for their wisdom and perspective on current events. Value their opinions, which have been shaped by years of experience.

Seek Help

Be realistic about the support you can give, and find other ways to fill in the gaps. Encourage your elderly loved one to attend a place of worship and participate in service or volunteer groups. Find a place where they can be part of a group of older people who travel together. Help them find ways to pursue hobbies they enjoy and develop new interests they never had time for. Include them in special events in your family, such as birthdays, holidays, graduations, and weddings.

Encourage spiritual growth. Spiritual health is a large part of emotional and mental well-being. Pray with them and for them. Give them books to read or books on tape to listen to that are affirming and encouraging. Get them large print religious books to facilitate reading. Membership in a religious community can provide a camaraderie of caring support to help them in challenging times.

The investment of time and energy you make to help enrich the lives of the elderly is an indication of the gratitude you have for your own life.

31 Correspond with Family Members

I write to you out of turn, and believe I must adopt the rule of only writing when I am written to, in hopes that may provoke more frequent letters.

—THOMAS JEFFERSON

A BABY BOOMER recently lamented that his sister had forgotten how to use a pen. "When she was in college, she would write absolutely wonderful and funny letters on pale pink onionskin sheets with little pink roses all over the background," he said. "Now I get a two-line, cyberspeak email—occasionally!"

Keeping in touch with immediate and extended family members is no less important to families now than it was a hundred years ago when letter writing and penmanship were considered critical personal skills. But life moves considerably faster today than it did even twenty years ago. Communication at every level has been abbreviated.

Today fewer and fewer people find time to write thank-you notes or small notes of encouragement to family and friends. Personal cell phones, email, and clever greeting cards have threatened to diminish our cultural capacity for crafting a personal message. Yet, in some measure, our ability to stay in touch with those we love has been enhanced by the emergence and affordability of communication technologies.

Personal phones, pagers, and email allow us to reach family and friends quickly. Instead of personal stationery and an occasional crossed-out word, our correspondence bears a favorite icon or signature and can be spell checked before pressing "send."

Keeping scattered families connected and involved in one another's lives is easier than ever before. Over one-third of the households in the United States now have internet access in their homes. A Pew study found that 104 million adults (more than half the U.S. population) was online last year, compared with 88 million earlier in the year. Three-quarters of those between the ages of eighteen and twenty-nine have internet access, with teenagers close behind at 73 percent. College freshmen today have been computer literate since they were in elementary school, if not before. While seniors (grandparents) were the group least likely to be online (just 15 percent of those over the age of sixty-five had internet access), nearly three in five online senior citizens (56 percent) say the internet has improved their connections with family.

What are we to make of these trends? Perhaps a good approach is to keep the old, traditional means of communication alive, and at the same time use all the technology available to stay in touch!

There are creative and fun ways to help your family reconnect and stay connected using both the internet and traditional mail. The end result is nearly always that children are able to make a closer connection to and have a stronger identity with extended family members. They also learn important social and communication skills as they write.

Family Reunions Online

The internet brings relatives on the other side of the globe to your desk or table. It enables instant communication at a tiny fraction of the cost of a telephone call. You can chat with your loved ones without having to comb your hair, spend time traveling, or consider time zones. Here are some suggestions:

1. Start a family memory book. Each week, one family member sends an email to the others with his or her favorite family memory. Other family members can add their memories of the event, ask questions, or just enjoy reading the message!

2. Gather recipes from family members online and compile them into a family recipe book.

3. Start a family discussion group via email. Choose a topic of common interest or just share concerns, prayer requests, and news.

4. Work together to begin tracing the family tree.

5. Establish a family web site. Even if you have never created a web page before, you can easily set up a family site if you have a little time and web access. If you have internet access, your hosting service likely provides you with space for your own personal web page and user-friendly online software to set it up. There are also numerous web sites that cater to family communication and offer free space and step-by-step help. Several services are available:

- A bulletin board for posting pictures, news, and announcements.
- Around-table discussion area.

- Scheduled private chat rooms for a *real* family reunion.
- A family calendar for birthdays, graduations, and special events.

Web sites like ComeHome.net (http://www.comehome.net/) and FamilyBuzz.com (http://www.familybuzz.com/) provide free private sites for families, as long as you are willing to tolerate the ever-present advertising and potential increase in junk email (spam) to all family members who use the site.

You might want to sponsor a family swap meet or garage sale on your web site or via a round-robin email. Each family lists their name, what they have to give away or swap (kids' clothes, old toys, videos, games, equipment, recipes), and what they need in return.

You might also want to create a special kids-only page on the family web site where cousins and other extended family members under a certain age can gather.

Don't Abandon the Personal Note

Handwritten notes, cards, and letters from those we love become cherished keepsakes. A rare handwritten note from a father, a grandchild's first thank-you note, the comforting and encouraging letter received during a rough patch, or a yellowing love letter—these tend to end up securely tucked away among treasured items.

When it's time to say "I'm sorry," add a few handwritten words of contrition before you sign that clever greeting card. Missing someone? Put it in ink, not in cyberspace.

You can help children develop an appreciation for handwritten letters and notes as well. Even before children can write, they can be encouraged to draw a thank-you note to a relative or family friend who has sent them a gift. Make the task as fun and easy as possible. "Thank you for the present."

"I love you, Grandma." "Please come visit us." These are eloquent missives when they are scrawled in red crayon. If help is needed with addressing the envelope, allow the child to place the stamp and put it in the mailbox.

Older children and teenagers may also need prompting to stay in touch with important people in their lives. You can give them silent encouragement in these ways:

- Set the example. Occasionally write your child a private note expressing pride in an accomplishment or encouragement when things are tough.
- Buy your child his or her own personal stationery.

Give your child a blank book to use as a diary to encourage writing skills.

32 Date Your Spouse

It's sad that children cannot know their parents when they were younger; when they were loving, courting, and being nice to one another. By the time children are old enough to observe, the romance has all too often faded or gone underground.

—Virginia Satir

IF YOU'VE BEEN MARRIED for a while, you may think there isn't anything about your husband or wife that you don't already know. You might be surprised to find out just how wrong you are!

Even childless couples find it easy to fall into a daily routine. Add the mix of children, schedules, work, lessons, extended family, religious practices, and community responsibilities, and most couples feel lucky to find ten or fifteen minutes of exclusive "us" time each day. Yet a marriage, like a car or the human body, needs attention and maintenance if it is to survive and thrive.

In today's busy world, couples have to be intentional about carving out exclusive time together. Falling into the same bed at the end of the day, with or without lovemaking, does not constitute exclusive time. While ten or fifteen minutes of conversation each day is important, it isn't nearly the amount of time you gave each other when you were dating!

Couples who decide to start dating again usually find that the guy or gal they fell in love with is still there—only better!

The Rules

To make dating work, you need to have a few ground rules so you and your spouse (as well as your family and friends) understand you are serious about carving out dating time.

1. Establish a fixed time and day. Pick a specific time every week when both of you are finished with work for the day. Once that time is established, don't make exceptions unless a true emergency arises.

2. No kids. No friends. No relatives. Be especially aware when kids try to manipulate you to include them in the date.

3. For the first few dates, pick a place neither of you has been before.

4. If you decide on a movie, concert, or the theater, make sure you have time for a meal together where you can just talk.

5. A quiet evening at home every now and then is great as long as the rest of the family is out for the evening or overnight. Plan something special—cook dinner together, rent an old movie, or play a board game.

6. Seriously limit the amount of time you spend talking about work.

7. Limit or entirely eliminate talk about family members, including your children.

8. Try to focus completely on each other as if you are two people on their first date.

What Will We Talk about If Not the Kids?

Here are some alternative conversation ideas:
- Share some of your deepest thoughts and feelings.
- Talk about your hopes and dreams for the future—perhaps even a fantasy or two. Share a list of things you want to do before you're fifty (or forty or sixty).
- Plan a romantic getaway, even if you think you won't really take it.
- Share a childhood secret you've never shared before.
- Plan your dream home as though you could afford anything, anywhere.
- Reminisce about your first date, your wedding, or some other special day.

Planning the Date

"Date night" needn't be night at all. A Saturday morning or Sunday afternoon date may be better if you or your spouse isn't a night person, or if you are both too tired from work to enjoy evening activities. The important thing is to choose a time when neither of you will be anxiously watching the clock.

When you were first dating, one date often ended with commitments or plans for the next date. Do the same now—talk about what you would like to do next week as you end the evening. Deciding what to do should never be a chore. What might you do besides try new restaurants? Here are some suggestions:
- Take a picnic to the park, lie on your back, and show each other pictures in the clouds (or stars).

- Go to a concert, dog show, or sports event that you both enjoy.
- Drive to a nearby town and go window-shopping.
- Go to a nearby lake or beach; take beach chairs and read to each other.
- Go to a special worship service or to hear a speaker that interests you both.
- Play golf, tennis, handball, or any other sport you enjoy. Choose something you can play with approximately the same skill level.
- Drive into the country and find a beautiful lane to wander down.
- Take a class together—such as a language, pottery, painting, or dance class.

Ultimately, you'll discover that your dates aren't really taking time away from your children or other obligations. To feel secure children need to see that their parents' relationship is solid. Parents who date are more likely to present a united front in decisions relating to the children.

It's an exciting and wonderful thing to experience the person you've been with for years as if for the very first time. Dating reconnects individuals in a marriage and awakens a spirit of excitement and intimacy in a relationship. It's almost like going back in time—a time when everything about the other person was new and interesting, when a quiet whisper sent chills down the spine, when kisses were soft and passionate. Remember a time when the most important thing in the world was the other person, when nothing else seemed to matter as long as you were together. Don't have any recent memories about such a time? Then you *especially* need to date your spouse!

33 Attend Family Events

> *My drawing was not a picture of a hat. It was a picture of a boa constrictor digesting an elephant. But since the grown-ups were not able to understand it, I made another drawing: I drew the inside of the boa constrictor so that the grown-ups could see it clearly. They always need to have things explained.*
>
> —Antoine de Saint-Exupery, *The Little Prince*

WHEN YOU ATTEND your child's opening night performance at a school play, you may very well think you're looking at a hat, when what you're supposed to see is a boa constrictor digesting an elephant. It's true—grown-ups sometimes need to have things explained. Even if you don't fully appreciate what you are seeing or hearing, your attendance at elementary school productions, dance and piano recitals, sporting events, art exhibits, and band and choir concerts is vital to your relationship to your child.

To communicate value and worth to your child, nothing is as affirming as a parent's undivided attention. Too often children are expected to live in the grown-ups' world. Getting into your child's world sends a message that he or she is important to you.

Become Your Child's Cheerleader

Children need the encouraging presence of their parents to give them confidence for that terrifying debut in a center stage solo performance, or to give them a competitive edge in the high hurdles. This is their opportunity to prove themselves with their skills and talents—their big moment to shine! They need to know they have done well and hear you say, "I am proud of you." When a child gives his or her best effort, parents should be there.

If the basketball game ends in a dismal loss, or well-rehearsed lines are forgotten in the panic of stage fright, parents can help the child learn how to maturely handle disappointment. Times of loss are great opportunities for saying to a child, "I love you no matter what—you can count on that!"

Encouragement or Pressure?

Knowing you will attend an event often motivates your child to work hard to perfect his skills and do his best in a performance. However, family support for a child's activities should never be so intense that it puts undue performance pressure on the child. Ask yourself, "Am I attending this event to support my child, or is my personal pride on the line? Do I see my child's performance as validating or impacting my own reputation?" If you answered yes to that last question, ask yourself, "Am I trying to live my life through my child?" That's a dangerous position to take—your child will not only feel intense pressure but will also feel even more of a failure if he doesn't do well. In the end, children resent parents who exert too much pressure to excel or win, and they can even sabotage their own performance in an effort to lessen the pressure in the future.

Never allow your anger to erupt at a child's performance, bully a coach or a child, issue demeaning insults, or hurl empty threats. Instead, be a voice of encouragement, enthusiasm, and support—not only for your child but also for all the children in the cast, on the team, or in the event.

Parent-Child Events

Besides being fans in the stands, parents give a great deal of support to their children by participating in parent-child events. Clubs and religious organizations often sponsor mother-daughter, mother-son, father-daughter, and father-son weekends or banquets to help develop and deepen one-on-one relationships between a parent and child. Participate as often as you can in these events!

Mother-daughter fashion shows and father-son golf tournaments are common parent-child activities. A mother's relationship with her daughter needs extra-sensitive care in the adolescent years. Look for activities to spend time together and keep the communication channels open.

Family experts also recognize the need to nurture mother-son and father-daughter relationships. Developing strong, positive mother-son relationships is particularly important in single-parent families that are often headed up by single women. A secure and trusting father-daughter relationship is critical as a girl enters her adolescent years.

Company-sponsored "Bring Your Child to Work" days help your children connect with your world and get a sense of what your work life is all about. You also get an opportunity to introduce your children to your boss and coworkers. Participating in "Bring Your Child to Work" days also shows the people you work with that your family is important to you.

Parents should also welcome their children's presence when they are recognized for professional or career accomplishments, or receive service awards in their workplace. Children get a good sense of the rewards of diligence and hard work, and gain pride in their parents.

Involve Other Children

Encourage your children to become enthusiastic fans of their siblings. Point out that every person has different talents and levels of skill. Applauding a sibling means applauding your family, even if that sibling is not the best player or performer.

As one woman noted, "My brother always applauded my piano concerts. I was a big fan at his baseball games. He didn't play the piano, and I don't play baseball—but we valued the other person's ability and willingness to participate. The fact is, I no longer perform on the piano and my brother no longer plays on a baseball team. Even so, we are still each other's biggest fans! He's quick to tell me about his successes, and I'm equally quick to tell him mine." By encouraging sibling applause and appreciation, you as a parent will be building a support system that your children can count on for many decades to come.

34 Organize Family Reunions

Call it a clan, call it a network, call it a tribe, call it a family. Whatever you call it, whoever you are, you need one.

—Jane Howard

FAMILY REUNIONS are as varied as families themselves! Whether a family gets together for Labor Day weekend, a vacation at the beach, or to celebrate a fiftieth anniversary, family reunions do have one thing in common—they nurture family relationships.

Get It Together!

The last century saw families moving from their hometowns to pursue work and career opportunities far away from loved ones. Children grew up hundreds of miles from their grandparents, aunts, and uncles. Cousins were strangers to one another. The desire to renew family connections has spurred recent growth and interest in family reunions. Newsletters, books, and web sites are devoted to all aspects of holding family reunions.

With participants spread around the globe, family reunions are a challenge to organize. Internet and email access are almost a must to keep the planning on track.

Start with a Committee

The starting point for a family reunion could be a special occasion (such as an eightieth birthday party), a rare visit from a family who lives overseas, or an annual event that takes place every Fourth of July. No matter what the occasion, the most effective way to get organized is to start with a committee. Without a committee the tasks will all fall to one person, who will probably never want to take on the challenge again!

If this is an annual event, rotate the planning responsibilities so everyone gets an opportunity to make decisions regarding time, location, food, theme, and activities.

Delegate Responsibilities

Once a committee has signed on to the idea, delegate responsibilities to task groups. Divide tasks into manageable responsibilities such as date, location, food, communication, entertainment, activities, and lodging. One person may also want to arrange for a photographer and a means to record the event, such as a scrapbook or a reunion-related video. Once tasks are assigned, develop a timeline when decisions need to be made and arrangements finalized.

Timing, Location, and Meal Planning

The date of the event is the first decision to make. If this is a first-time effort, poll the participants for preferred dates, locations, and activities. The determining factors should be (1) when the most people can attend, and (2) what activities are preferred, such as skiing, boating, or playing baseball. Once the date is decided, give plenty of advance notice to ensure the greatest turnout.

The location of the reunion is an important decision. Make a list of the facilities that will be needed—such as a restaurant, park, campground, hall, or hotel, and an estimated size of the gathering and budget constraints. The location subcommittee should then search for a suitable site that fits the agreed-upon price range. A location that is central and accessible to the most people will draw the best turnout.

Feeding a crowd takes planning. Restaurants, potlucks, barbecues, catering, and home cooking are options for meals. If a kitchen is available, try serving favorite family recipes. Cooking together provides a good shared experience for the family cooks.

Recreation and Reminiscence

To facilitate interaction at the reunion, designate an activities committee. Not all the children will be excited about spending a few days with strangers; planned group activities will help pull them together. Recreation is a good way to get everyone participating. How about a tug-of-war or baseball game between generation groups, or a cousins' volleyball game? Consider hiring a recreation director to organize fun activities for the children. Make this a positive time for family members of all ages.

Reunions are an opportunity to reminisce. Bring old family photos from holidays and weddings and have a place to post them. Bring an heirloom with a family story to tell. Set up a place to display the items and plan a time to share their history.

Devise a trivia contest with a prize for the winner. Here are some sample questions:

- Where did Grandma and Grandpa meet?
- What are their middle names?
- Who came the longest distance to attend the reunion?
- Who looks most like Grandma? Grandpa? Aunt Evelyn? Uncle Johann?
- What characteristics have been passed on through the generations—big feet? Red hair? Brown eyes? Musical talent? A gap-toothed grin?

Hire a photographer to take the family photo. Post the time of the picture taking to get as many people as possible in the photo.

Family reunions are often remembered for renewing family bonds. They help pass on family legacies to future generations.

35 Pray for Your Family

Why leave your child's life to chance when you can give it to God?

—STORMIE OMARTIAN

IT'S HARD TO TRUST anyone else with the well-being of your family—even if that someone else is God! But it doesn't take long for parents to realize that they can't provide *everything* their children need, and they can't be with their children to protect them *everywhere* they go. Successful parenting takes more than good parents!

Parents can influence their children's destiny through prayer. Many famous people (Abraham Lincoln, John Wesley, Oral Roberts, and Franklin Graham) tribute their success to the prayers of a loving parent.

We're Only Human!

One authority has noted that people become parents the moment they realize life is out of their control—they are now intricately and intimately involved with another person with a will of his or her own. That's a scary thought when we consider our own shortcomings and areas of weakness!

How do you bridge the gap between what your child needs and what you as an imperfect human being can give your child? The answer is prayer, and lots of it!

Prayer Resources

There are great resources available to help us pray for our families, including books, conferences, tapes, magazines, prayer groups, and sacred religious writings. For example, the Bible is a great prayer book. Many of the verses can be turned into prayers. You might pray Philippians 4:13 for your child—that she will know God's strength to do all things that God wants her to do. Share that verse with your child to express that she is not expected to be able to do everything alone.

You might also pray Psalm 23:1 for your child—that he will be guided all day by God. Share that verse with your child to let him know God is with him no matter what circumstance or situation he finds himself in.

Be Specific

Everything is important to God—there is nothing that doesn't concern him about you or your child. When you pray for your family, be specific. Make a list of each family member's needs and challenges and ask God to meet those needs.

Pray with steadfastness and perseverance. As a parent you will never reach a time when you have prayed everything there is to pray for your children. That doesn't mean your prayers aren't being answered, but your children—no matter how old they are—will always need your prayers! Even when your prayers seem ineffective, keep on praying. Faithful prayer brings results. God is always working.

Prayer for the protection of a child is perhaps the most urgent request a parent has, especially when a teenager begins to drive or date. Pray that the psalmist's words would be true for your child: "For [God] will command his angels concerning you to guard you in all your ways; they will lift you up in their hands, so that you will not strike your foot against a stone" (Psalm 91:11–12). Letting go of a child as he or she grows up is always difficult for a parent. But trusting God to be there for your child helps you make those necessary transitions!

Pray to Become God's Person

One of the most important prayers parents can pray is that their children will become the people God created them to be. God's purposes and plans for your children exceed even yours! In becoming the person God created, your child will have every blessing God planned for his or her life. The Bible says, "We know that all things work together for good to those who love God, who have been called according to his purpose" (Romans 8:28). Parents can get discouraged by the way things appear in their child's life, but even those things that cause frustration or pain can be used for good.

Don't forget to also pray for your spouse and marriage. If you are a single parent, pray all the more! According to Tom Albin, author of *Teach Us to Pray*, "Being a single parent is the most difficult job in the world. Without prayer it can never be accomplished."

Most of all, be an example of prayer to your child. Let him know your love goes beyond the cares of this world and this life—that your desire is for his well-being for all eternity. Your prayers may be the most important contribution you can make to your child's life!

36 Pray with Your Family

He who has learned to pray has learned the greatest secret of a holy and happy life.

—WILLIAM LAW

PRAYING TOGETHER has many benefits for your family, according to Tom Albin, dean of the Upper Room Chapel in Nashville, Tennessee. Albin says, "Praying together is the only way to create memories and patterns that will help our children and grandchildren have the rich, joyful prayer life that God intends for them to have."

Albin says children learn to pray by praying with others. It is the same way they learn to cook, read, or develop other skills—by watching someone else and doing it together. Praying together as a family also strengthens the bonds that keep families close.

Growing through Family Prayer

Praying together gives children a model for handling difficulties. By sharing concerns—a hard day at work, a grandparent who is ill, a friend who was injured on the playground—a child learns positive ways to respond to everyday situations. Begin praying together now, before problems arise. Then you will have a resource in place when difficulties develop.

When families pray together they learn compassion for those outside their family. They share in the needs of others—first in prayer and then in "putting feet to prayers" by responding to those needs. Cheri Fuller, founder of Families Pray USA, has said that when children have a chance to help, they don't feel quite as helpless. After praying about a situation, explore with your child some ways he or she can help bring hope to a difficult situation.

Pray through the News

Pray also for the situations and people you read or hear about in the news. Fuller recommends watching the news together and then praying about the situation at hand, for the president and other political leaders, and for those who are trying to help. With catastrophes such as the World Trade Center bombings, pray repeatedly with your children but avoid overexposing them to graphic and traumatizing news reports.

Fuller suggests that children make "prayer stations" to remind them to pray. Cut out newspaper articles or collect photos of those who need prayer. Mount and post the clippings around your home and go from station to station praying for each individual.

Keep a globe available so children can learn where events are taking place. If your religious group supports missionaries around the world, a globe will also remind families to pray for them. Keep a list of the missionaries and where they are located. Have your name added to their email lists so you will be notified of immediate requests that need prayer. Involve your children in praying for them.

Children at a church in Tulsa, Oklahoma, prayed for the safe release of kidnapped missionary Bruce Olsson who was being held hostage in South America. Weeks after his release, Olsson was a guest speaker in their church. He told about the kidnapping, his witness to his captors, and God's faithfulness to him. Children learned a lesson in prayer that they will never forget!

Prayer Mates

Encourage children to pray with and for their siblings. Praying for one another develops compassion and care for the other person. In praying together as children, siblings bond as prayer buddies interceding for one another. Those early habits and practices of prayer will help forge good relationships that can last through the years.

Pray together as a couple. Become a true soul mate with your spouse. A couple who prays together grows in unity, trust, and mutual respect. Prayer enhances intimacy with God and one another. When you face a problem, turn together in prayer to seek God's solutions. The divorce rate in America is tragically high, but statistics show that couples that *pray* together tend to *stay* together.

Teaching children to pray—and praying together as a family—is a legacy parents can give to their children. Learning by doing is a lesson that will not be soon forgotten!

37 Plant a Memorial Tree

He who plants a tree plants a hope.

—Lucy Larcom

SYMBOLIC TREE-PLANTING ceremonies are an age-old ritual in many countries and in numerous cultures and religions. Putting a healthy young tree into the ground is a symbol of celebration that represents life, hope, growth, and continuity.

Planting a tree is a wonderful gift to honor an event or person. Trees are often planted to commemorate important family occasions:

- Births
- Graduations
- Bar or Bat Mitzvahs
- Easter
- Weddings
- Anniversaries
- Mother's Day
- Father's Day

You might also plant a tree to celebrate these special events:

- The start of a new friendship
- The beginning of a new job

- The retirement of a family member
- The death of a beloved pet
- Recovery from a long or serious illness
- The purchase of your first home
- The establishment of a new business or partnership
- A child's first day of school
- A child's first communion or confirmation

Planting the Tree

Choose a location where you and your family can watch the tree grow. If you are planting in a park or other public area, be sure to get permission from park or city officials or landowners before proceeding.

When planting in your own yard, place trees that memorialize family members where they can be seen from a window. Ask your local greenhouse to help you select a tree that will thrive in the area you have chosen. Take the family to select the tree. Remember that an evergreen will be green all year, but deciduous trees have beautiful fall color. Keep in mind the occasion or person being honored as you make your selection.

Whether a joyful celebration or a sad commemoration, make the tree-planting a family event. If you are memorializing a loved one, allow each person to help place the tree in the prepared hole and then shovel a scoop of dirt around the tree. A small ritual surrounding the planting can bring comfort to the family. Once the tree is securely in the ground, seal the occasion by having family members tell why they were thankful for the life of the honoree and perhaps say a prayer.

Commemorate the planting by taking pictures, especially if the tree is planted where your family will see it only occasionally. Use the pictures to help track the tree's growth.

Remember to tend the tree as it grows. If it can be seen from the street, consider decorating it for holidays. If it is a memorial tree, tie a yellow ribbon around the trunk or hang yellow ribbons from the branches on the honoree's birthday.

Timing

While trees are most often planted in the spring, there is really no time of year in the United States when trees may not be planted. As long as the ground is not too cold and the saplings have been outside, everything should turn out fine.

Many families enjoy buying a live Christmas tree each year and planting it in the spring. Since evergreens are long-lived, their presence can enhance the beauty and value of the property. A word of caution: don't plant one year's tree too close to last year's. One tree could encroach upon another, necessitating its removal.

No Yard?

If you live in a city where planting spots are hard to come by, there are nonprofit organizations that will plant the tree for you and send a card to the honoree or his family to notify them of your gift. Some of these organizations are engaged in global reforestation. That means your gift of one tree is matched by one to twenty-five trees planted in the United States or other countries where fires or overharvesting have endangered the natural environment. Gifts to nonprofit organizations are tax deductible, so consider planting more than one tree!

Before you decide, check out several tree-planting organizations. The location of the trees, the purpose of the organizations, the honoree acknowledgments, the types of services offered, and the prices vary greatly (generally from $2.95 per tree to over $50).

38 Handle Money Wisely

Debt is no man's friend; it will always make you a slave.

—RON AND JUDY BLUE

FINANCIAL RESPONSIBILITY is a difficult job. It's a must, however, if you want your family to have everything it needs. Decide that you *are* going to provide adequately for your children and that you *will* exemplify good provision of a parent for a child.

Poverty is considered the foremost reason for a variety of society's ills, not the least of which are the bad health of children and adults who live in poverty. It is also partially to blame for the low educational scores and levels of education attained by poor children and teens. In turn, poor health and low school achievement tend to result in lower-paying jobs. Crime and racial tension have also been associated with poverty.

Issues related to money are considered the number-one cause of conflict in marriage, and also the number-one cause of frustration in families as a whole. A family that doesn't have enough money to buy the basics—food, shelter, adequate clothing, and school supplies—can feel ashamed and worthless.

For a family to be financially strong, economists agree that three issues must be addressed: debt, insurance, and retirement planning.

Freedom from Debt

One of the greatest freedoms you can give your children is freedom from debt, especially credit card and term-payment debt. Being debt free enables a family to invest in more educational opportunities, enriching travel experiences, faith-based outreach to others, and the dreams of owning a business or starting a nonprofit fund.

To achieve freedom from debt, a family needs to do four things:

1. Avoid all impulse buying.
2. Limit spending to basic needs only.
3. Invest time and energy into finding creative, low-cost forms of recreation and entertainment.
4. Set a family goal of paying off all outstanding debt—and set a time frame for achieving this goal. Decide on a family reward that you will receive when you are free of debt.

Dave Ramsey, author of the best-selling *Financial Peace*, advocates "dumping debt" by moving to a pay-cash basis for all purchases (except business travel, for which he uses a debit card), and simultaneously paying into an emergency fund until $1,000 is in that account.

Once this amount is in place as a backup fund, Ramsey recommends that you no longer use any credit cards and that balances on existing cards be paid using a "snowball" technique—paying the minimum on all cards except the credit card on which the interest is highest. On that account, pay as much as possible until the card is paid in full. Then the amount of money that was being allocated to that card should be applied to the debt with the next highest interest rate, and so forth until all credit cards are paid.

As soon as credit cards are paid in full, Ramsey recommends using the amount once paid on credit card purchases toward a more rapid payoff of house and automobile loans.[1]

Adequate Insurance

Parents with young and school-age children should seriously consider having life and disability insurance. In the event of a parent's death, serious accident, or disabling illness, insurance can mean the difference between providing an adequate lifestyle and education for your children, and thrusting your survivors into poverty. Make sure you have insurance to cover both parents, especially if both parents are providing income.

A Sound Retirement Plan

Plan for your elderly years while you can! Sadly, a significant number of elderly people live at or near poverty because they relied too much upon government Social Security payments after retirement. Take charge of your own retirement planning.

Make certain any contributions you make to a retirement fund associated with your employer are invested in a varied portfolio, with an emphasis on mutual funds that routinely perform well. Make additional payments on a monthly basis to your own retirement plan. Be sure to take advantage of retirement plans that allow you to use pre-tax dollars, such as IRAs. If you plan for your retirement years, you have a much greater opportunity to give *yourself* the life you want to have as an older person.

Become Informed

If you don't know how to establish a good retirement plan or how to manage your money wisely, don't be embarrassed—seek out a financial advisor. A number of advisory groups are available through various community agencies. Many of them are staffed by retired accountants and money managers who volunteer their services.

Paying Child Support

If you are separated from your children through divorce and are required to pay child support, *never* miss a payment! Make child support a priority. If for some reason you don't know the whereabouts of your child, make monthly payments into a fund. Your child may seek you out some day, and having a fund available at that time will be a tangible expression of your ongoing love and concern. Such a fund can bring genuine restoration and the renewal of a relationship.

39 Exercise Together

Exercise and application produce order in our affairs, health of body, cheerfulness of mind, and these make us precious to our friends.

—Thomas Jefferson

PHYSICAL EDUCATION is no longer a standard part of the curriculum in many public schools. Rather, physical fitness has been relegated to the realm of extracurricular activities and organized sports. While the United States *appears* to be crazed with working out, the fact is today's young people are less fit, more obese, and less inclined to engage in aerobic exercise than the young people of the previous generation.

One of the best things you can do for your family is to exercise together. The American Heart Association offers these tips for raising heart-healthy children:

• Make sure leisure time includes physical activity for every member of the family.

• When your child is bored, suggest something that gets her moving, such as playing catch in the yard or building a snowman.

- Help set fitness goals for your child—community "fun runs" for children are good motivators for accomplishing goals.
- Choose a fitness-oriented gift for your child, such as a jump rope, tennis racket, or baseball bat.
- Look for clubs in your area that offer sports and lessons in activities your child enjoys. Many city recreational departments provide free opportunities for involvement in sports, such as soccer and softball leagues for both boys and girls.

Seven Areas of Benefit

Family exercise affords these important benefits:

1. *Better family health.* The benefits of exercise can be experienced by both parent and child—greater strength, flexibility, endurance, cardiovascular health, and improved resistance to disease and injury. Those who exercise generally experience fewer missed days of work or school, greater productivity, higher grades, and greater alertness and mental quickness in decision making and problem solving. The benefits of exercise are physical, mental, emotional, and relational.

2. *Greater health awareness.* The more your child pursues physical fitness, the greater the likelihood he or she will shun junk food, cigarettes, alcohol, and drugs.

3. *More talk time.* Exercising together gives time for parent-child talk—even if it is while you both soak in a whirlpool *after* a workout.

4. *Greater personal discipline.* Setting aside regular exercise times each week instills personal discipline as well as time management skills. Be an example by always keeping the exercise appointments you set with your child.

5. *Better sleep.* Those who exercise regularly often experience better sleep patterns. A well-rested child usually has a

more pleasant temperament and scores better academically than children who don't get enough exercise.

6. *Structured time together.* For parents who want to spend more quality time with their children, exercise is a perfect solution. Even if nothing profound is said or done during a workout, children rely on exercise sessions as a time when their parent is totally available for one-on-one communication.

7. *A spirit of cooperation.* Exercising together affords a good opportunity for a parent to encourage a child to develop co-operative skills—communication, mutual decision making, problem solving, and support of others. If your teenager is spotting for you as you lift weights, he becomes a partner in a mutually agreed-upon goal.

Playing Sports Together

Families can build team spirit by playing sports together. Sports activities are an excellent way to teach children the following:

- *Rules of a game or sport.* Even a quick game of basketball, tag football, or soccer can be an opportunity to teach your child the basic rules or skills associated with a particular game.

- *Principles of fair play.* Don't allow your child to cheat in a practice setting—what a child does in practice, she is also likely to do in an official game.

- *Gracious winning and losing.* Teach your child to congratulate winners with a hearty "Way to go!" and a genuine compliment on their good play. Teach your winning child to say, "I enjoyed our game" upon receiving congratulations from others.

- *Competing without malice.* Don't allow your child to become overly angry or upset at competitors. Keep the game friendly.

- *Playing without injury.* Insist that your play be in a safe area—no broken bottles, stones, or dangerous objects—and that any protective gear appropriate to the sport be worn by all family members.
- *Team morale and cooperation.* Teach your child how to cheer on other team members and to cooperate fully in plays called by the coach.
- *The fun of team play.* Encourage your child to have fun. Put your emphasis on the fact that you have played together, rather than on who won or lost.

Younger children who play sports with older siblings learn a key principle of life: skills are often directly related to physical maturity. Height, strength, overall size, agility, and speed factor into virtually every sport! On the other hand, enthusiasm is also a key ingredient in playing and winning at sports. Even young children can be taught to cheer on fellow teammates and play to their maximum ability.

Older children who play sports with younger siblings also learn an important lesson—helping rather than ridiculing weaker or younger players can raise the overall success of the team. Older players should be quick to coach, encourage, and protect younger players.

Find a Mutually Enjoyable Exercise or Sport

Find something that both you and your child enjoy playing or doing.
- Walk, jog, or ride bicycles.
- Play a round of golf together.
- Swim or take a water aerobics class.
- Join a multigenerational aerobics dance class.
- Go bowling as a family.
- Go on a hike through a wilderness area or state park.

40 Volunteer Together

Do all the good you can, by all the means you can, in all the ways you can, in all the places you can, at all the times you can, to all the people you can, as long as ever you can.

—JOHN WESLEY

VOLUNTEERING ENGAGES FAMILY members in a cooperative activity that is meaningful and personally fulfilling. The best volunteer activities emphasize three things:

- *Equality.* Each person in the family becomes an equally vital contributor to the success of the project.
- *Equanimity.* Volunteering is an activity that has no winners or losers, but rather requires cooperation and a positive attitude.
- *Experience.* Those who volunteer together learn the roles of leader and follower. They learn to submit to authority and follow instructions from a variety of leaders using different leadership styles.

Benefits of Volunteering

Volunteer activities often provide opportunities to develop new skills, especially if the task involves construction, warehousing and inventory processes, or medical assistance.

A volunteer project can also give these six benefits to your family:
- Structured time together
- Topics for family conversation that are purposeful and help develop decision-making and problem-solving skills
- Opportunities to make new friends
- Opportunities to see new places and be exposed to new environments
- Chances to explore possible career interests of your children
- Feelings of service and contribution that translate into feelings of self-worth and value

Decide as a Family

Make the volunteering decision one that involves all family members. Discuss areas of mutual interest or perceived need. Ask yourselves these questions:
- What unmet need do we recognize in our neighborhood, community, or faith group?
- What might we do as a family to help meet this need?
- What commitment on our part is required?

Consider various options for meeting a need. For example, helping to feed the homeless may mean participating in a canned-food drive, ladling soup or handing out sandwiches at a feeding center, or delivering sacks of groceries at holiday times.

Weigh the various options against current family commitments and schedules. You may not be able to immediately participate to the level you desire. If that's the case, set a family goal of making yourselves more available for volunteer work in the future.

Here or There?

Start with a local volunteer project. The best place to serve is in your immediate community or city. That's the place where you are most likely to see results and make an ongoing contribution, as opposed to a one-time gift of your time and talent.

If you enjoy volunteering as a family on a local scale, consider taking a vacation that includes volunteer service—perhaps to help those in a needy area of the nation or even to work in a needy area overseas. Religious organizations often provide opportunities to volunteer at service centers or mission stations around the world. Participating in programs with people of like beliefs is usually a good way for families to feel connected to other volunteers. This is a great way for children to make friends with a shared faith.

Organized Charitable Group or Family-Initiated?

Activities organized by volunteer groups are often the most convenient for a family participation. However, some charitable organizations have age restrictions. For example, young children may not be welcome at a Habitat-for-Humanity building site. It may not be appropriate to take young children to drug or alcohol rehabilitation centers. Ask these questions as you communicate with an organization:

- What activities are available for volunteers?
- Is there something for every member of our family to do?
- Do we need to have any prerequisite skills or information?
- What should we wear and bring at the time we volunteer our service?

Not all volunteer activities need to be planned by established charitable organizations. One parent who was homeschooling her three children scheduled at least one family concert at a nursing home each month. The children learned songs and developed a program to share with residents. The activity cheered the listeners and the children benefited from learning and rehearsing new music, creating their own choreography and costumes, and developing performance skills.

Long-Term or Short-Term Involvement?

Not all volunteer activities require a long-term commitment. Often, however, it is wise and rewarding to offer a long season of service. This will instill in your children an opportunity to see that many needs are ongoing, and therefore ongoing service is required to meet them. Repeated volunteer service or several months of committed service also helps a child become comfortable with a volunteer setting or activity, which is likely to translate into a greater willingness to volunteer in the future.

Parent-Child Teams

At times, interest in volunteering may be effective in strengthening mother-daughter or father-son relationships. Explore those possibilities, especially if you feel as a parent that you aren't spending enough time with one of your children.

A mother-daughter activity might be a quilting group that makes quilts for missionaries. Such an activity provides meaningful mother-daughter interaction and exposes a girl to other mothers and daughters of similar commitment and interest.

A father-son activity might involve planting trees or turning a vacant lot into a place where kids can play basketball or handball. Again, such an activity not only provides meaningful father-son time together but also gives a boy an opportunity to see how other fathers and sons interact.

41 Create a Positive Family Atmosphere

Feelings of worth can flourish only in an atmosphere in which individual differences are appreciated, love is shown openly, mistakes are used for learning, communication is open, rules are flexible, responsibility (matching promise with delivery) is modeled and honesty is practiced—the kind of atmosphere found in a nurturing family.

—Virginia Satir

ONE OF THE BEST THINGS you can do for your family is avoid negativity! It is highly destructive to family security, strength, and harmony. Recognize negative statements and attitudes as "family poisons," and refuse to allow them to infect your family!

Avoid Gossip

The old adage, "If you can't say something nice, don't say anything at all" is still good wisdom for today! Don't engage in idle, opinion-based speculation about what a person has done or said, or the motivation underlying the behavior. Deal with facts. If something isn't your business, don't make it your business. No person ever knows the *whole* truth about another person, and no gossip is ever acting for the good of another person. Gossip nearly always tears down reputations, including that of the gossip himself. Don't set that example for your children!

Eliminate Negative Talk

When you ask your child or spouse about the events of their day, frame your questions in a positive way:
- What was the best thing about your day?
- Which part of today was good enough to repeat?
- What positive thing did you learn today?
- What did you see that was beautiful today?

Listen closely to the answers you are given and ask positive follow-up questions. Be prepared to share with your child or spouse the positive things about your own day.

If your child criticizes himself, perhaps calling himself stupid, dumb, or a failure, point out that this is not how *you* see him. Remind him that his performance on any given day is not the sum of who he is or can be. Ask your child, "What are you going to do to become smarter, wiser, or more successful? What are you going to do to activate your *real* potential?"

Put a Stop to All Forms of Abuse

Abuse is often thought of only in terms of physical or sexual mistreatment. Abuse can also involve neglect or emotional cruelty. A list of abuse criteria is provided below:
- *Physical abuse:* evidence of bruises and welts, burns (especially those related to hot liquids, cigarettes, rope, and pat-

terns made by a hot item), fractures, lacerations and abrasions, and human bite marks.
- *Sexual abuse:* fondling, sodomy, or intercourse between an adult and child.
- *Neglect:* consistently dirty, unwashed, hungry, or inappropriately dressed children; being left alone without supervision for extended periods of time in dangerous situations; unattended physical problems or lack of routine medical care; exploitation for financial gain; keeping a child from school; abandonment.

Two categories of neglect are recognized by our nation's court system but often overlooked by parents. The first is *moral* neglect—a failure to teach basic principles of right and wrong. The second is *psychological* neglect—a failure to provide for a child's basic psychological growth and development.

- *Emotional maltreatment:* constantly blaming or belittling a child; portraying a cold and rejecting attitude; withholding love; treating siblings unequally; showing a lack of concern about the child's problems.

No form of abuse has a rightful place in a family or anywhere else! If you are the victim of physical or sexual abuse, you need to tell authorities about what you have experienced. That way you will bring justice to your abuser and protect others in close proximity to him or her. In cases where a statute of limitations keeps you from experiencing legal justice, you should still seek out counselors or religious authorities who can help you achieve a sense of justice through psychological and social means.

Avoid Long Periods of Silence or Separation

When dealing with conflicts, don't avoid communication—that only makes things worse. Hurt feelings rot into bitterness; grievances stew into hatred. Time doesn't heal—it only delays response. Children interpret silence or separation from a parent as rejection and a withdrawal of love. Keep the communication flowing, even if it isn't pleasant.

Create a Climate for Listening

Be committed to listening to your children and spouse with an open heart. Listening takes time, and your time is deeply desired by your family members. Listening creates a climate of trust. Listening to what your child is thinking will help you know if you are instilling the value-rich behavior and positive attitudes you desire to see in your child.

Model Behavior You Want to See

Positive climates produce positive people. A home with a positive atmosphere is not just a nice place to live—it is a productive, effective training field for instilling attitudes and behavior you want to see in your children. If you want your child to pursue their potential, pursue *your* potential! If you want your child to believe that family is special, express that *you* believe your family is special. If you want to instill flexibility, responsiveness, and a can-do attitude in your child, *exhibit* flexibility, responsiveness, and a can-do attitude. Choose to embody the traits you desire to see in your child.

42 Teach Children to Budget

Economy does not lie in sparing money, but in spending it wisely.

—THOMAS HENRY HUXLEY

CHILDREN ARE SMARTER and richer today than kids were twenty years ago, but they still need guidance on how to spend money. As soon as children are old enough to understand and use money (generally ages three to eight), they are ready for a budget.

Dividing the Money

Begin with a simple three-jar or three-envelope strategy. Label them "Giving," "Saving," and "Spending."

Spend a few minutes telling your child why you have each jar or envelope. Talk about the importance of giving and saving money. Use illustrations that he or she can relate to.

A young child who doesn't seem to understand the concepts of saving and giving may be too young to start this process. In that case, use one envelope, placing the money in it in small denominations. If you are giving her five dollars, put five ones in the envelope so it becomes more empty when she spends instead of fuller (with more bills from change). Children also need a basic understanding of the relative value of bills and coins even if they don't yet understand the mathematics involved.

Periodically give your young child three coins (or three bills) and instruct him to put one in each container. At about six or seven years of age, children are ready to understand simple divisions. For example, the smallest part of their money might go to giving, the largest part to savings, and the rest to spending. In the beginning you may need to help them comprehend this process. Be sure your kids are given their money in a way that allows them to divide it easily. For example, ten dollars could easily be divided into ten one-dollar bills, with one dollar for giving, five dollars for savings, and four dollars for spending.

Always allow the child to physically put the money in the jar or envelope, even if you have to help with the amounts.

Next, help the child make his first budget. At this level the only thing that needs to be written down is the savings goal. The object of this goal should be saving for something the child will be able to afford *soon*. However, the item should be more expensive than what he can buy with his remaining spending money.

Let Children Participate in Family Budgeting

As children get older and begin earning money from odd jobs and babysitting, they are ready to create a more complex budget for their money. They are also ready to be active participants in the family budgeting process. A good way to introduce ten- to twelve-year-olds to the household budget is to have them help you write the monthly checks. A little check-writing instruction and a few seconds to double-check their work before you sign the check is all it will take.

Now is also a good time to demonstrate to your children your own commitment to giving. Let the child assist you in calculating what your family's gift should be, and let her write that check first. This process helps teach a child that sharing doesn't just mean giving away what's left over, but intentionally giving the first slice of the pie as an act of compassion.

You may feel that helping your children understand the family budget is a useless exercise, since you barely understand it yourself! But there are many tools available to help you, and you may be surprised at how well your child grasps the process. For instance, the web site TheFamily.com has a page called "Family Budget Calculator," a free, interactive budget planner. Armed with your paycheck stub, housing and utility bills, and credit card bills, you can easily develop a family budget. Although it's not a secure site, use of the page is anonymous and figures you enter are not related to personal information. The site is a good place to demonstrate how a budget works to children who are eight and older.

Whether you choose to use a software program, an online service, or a calculator and spreadsheet, allow your child to enter the numbers and help calculate the monthly budget. Encourage your child to make a budget sheet for his or her own earnings.

From the time children begin to earn their own money, they need to see themselves as part of the family financial picture. While they may think that paying for their food and clothing is strictly Mom and Dad's problem, they adopt a more realistic view when they are part of financial decisions.

For instance, allow them to help plan a family vacation and write the budget. Then assign them to help keep track of the family's spending as the vacation progresses. While planning, ask them to suggest several destinations and do comparative research on the costs of each place.

Children who are taught to budget and have participated in family budget decisions are still likely to want the latest fad or expensive gadget. They are, however, also likely to present you with a plan for acquiring it when they ask. Kids who have actively participated in making budgets are also more likely to resist the lure of credit card company offers—or, at least, to use credit wisely. In 1997, a staggering 67 percent of college students had credit cards with an average balance of $1,879, and 10 percent had balances exceeding $7,000, according to a Nellie Mae report.[1]

43 Worship as a Family

It is only when men begin to worship that they begin to grow.

—CALVIN COOLIDGE

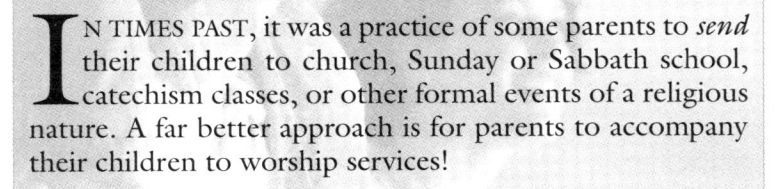

IN TIMES PAST, it was a practice of some parents to *send* their children to church, Sunday or Sabbath school, catechism classes, or other formal events of a religious nature. A far better approach is for parents to accompany their children to worship services!

Start Young

Don't wait until your child is in school to expose him or her to religious services. Most houses of worship have childcare. As quickly as possible, however, include your child in the regular service. Your child will benefit from learning rituals associated with worship, hearing teachings and music, seeing dramatic presentations, and learning liturgy.

Even young children who cannot sing along can enjoy beautiful stained glass windows and the opportunity to be in a familiar group of adults and older children.

Choose a Family Emphasis

Choose a house of worship that has a strong emphasis on the family. If your place of worship doesn't have a family program, talk to your pastor, priest, rabbi, or worship leader about developing programs for children and youth. Look for these things:

• *Religious education.* Is religious education provided for children of all ages? Check out the curriculum being used. Does it teach the values you are trying to instill in your child? Does it have the potential to be challenging and motivating?

• *Choirs and musical training for children and teens.* Are opportunities provided for your child to join musical groups with other youth? Will your child be able to sing, play an instrument, participate in liturgical dance classes, or join a handbell choir? Are opportunities provided for your child to participate in pageants, dramatic skits, or other performance programs?

• *Ministry or special growth opportunities for young people.* A number of houses of worship have clubs for children and teens. Some have outreach programs that routinely involve young people—from ladling soup to homeless families to helping with yard work and housekeeping for elderly members. Some churches provide opportunities for young people to participate in the service itself—they can light candles, read Scripture, or play in an orchestra. Ask about opportunities for your child to be of service to the place of worship as well as to the community.

Attend Regularly

Your child will feel connected to a church and its youth-related programs only if he or she attends regularly. Make attendance a normal part of each week's schedule.

Make Youth Group a Priority

Most houses of worship have a teen youth group that meets weekly, and sometimes opportunities are also available for interdenominational or interfaith youth programs. (For example, Young Life is for high school students of all Christian denominations.) Ask questions of the youth leader. What does a normal youth group meeting include? Are outings or social activities scheduled periodically? Does the youth group participate in camps or retreat programs?

Socialize with Other Families in Your Faith Community

Seek out families from your place of worship whose children are close in age to your own. Invite these families to your home. You might also plan picnics or swim parties, attend a concert in a nearby city, or plan other social outings together. Get to know people who have shared values, concerns, and spiritual commitments. Build ongoing friendships with families that fit comfortably with your family—parents with like interests, and children of similar ages and interests.

In doing this you establish a peer group for your child. Children and teens make friends with whom they can attend religious events. They have a growing sense of community in which they feel safety, freedom to express themselves, and full acceptance. A teenager who has at least one friend of similar faith background is often able to withstand a tremendous amount of peer pressure from friends who have little or no faith commitment.

Create a Home Atmosphere of Worship

Children learn much about prayer and praise within the family context. Be quick to consult your faith's religious writings when a question arises about God, religion, or an ethical issue. Make prayer a part of your family routine. Encourage your child to read sacred writings. Give each child copies of important religious works as gifts. Use children's versions of sacred writings to familiarize your child with the history or beliefs of your faith. Voice praise to God for the good things you experience. Instill in your child awareness that God is always present, listening, and worthy of thanksgiving.

Set Spiritual Goals

What spiritual goals do you have for each of your children? Give thought to what you hope your child will be spiritually. Express your desires to him or her. In *Building Strong Families*, Dr. William Mitchell advocates these values and traits as goals parents might set for their children:[1]

- *Faith in God*—specifically a faith that is actively incorporated into daily conversations, habits, and decisions
- *Hope*—an expectation that good will always prevail over evil, and that God reigns supreme in all things
- *Integrity*—a seamless harmony in what a child believes, says, and does
- *Love for others*—marked by generous giving
- *Truthfulness*—even when the immediate consequences may be unpleasant
- *Joy*—a bright optimism that God is working all things to an eternally good outcome
- *Peace*—an inner contentment that God is in control
- *Courage*—to confront evil in appropriate ways
- *Self-control*—an inner fortitude to say "Yes" to good and "No" to evil
- *Patience*—to be patient with people and irksome situations

44 Do Home Chores Together

Nothing is particularly hard if you divide it into small jobs.

—Mark Twain

EVERY PERSON IN A FAMILY should have responsibility for the upkeep and maintenance of the family home. When a person is responsible for cleaning and refurbishing a space, that person tends to feel more responsible not only for keeping the space clean but also greater responsibility for the family as a whole.

Responsible for Personal Space and Clothing

All family members should be responsible, to some degree, for cleaning their rooms and taking care of their clothing. Even young children can be taught to put dirty garments in a clothes hamper or take them to a laundry room basket. Older children can run loads of laundry in a washing machine and iron wrinkled garments.

Children should be taught to make their beds and to keep their rooms free of clutter. You can help them by supplying sufficient closet, drawer, or storage space for clothes, toys, and school supplies. If possible, make certain that each school-aged child has a desk and reading lamp.

Even young children can help pick up their toys at the end of a day. Older children should be taught to dust, vacuum, sweep, mop, and clean the windows and mirrors in their room.

Young children can also help with emptying wastepaper baskets, making sure all bathrooms are sufficiently stocked with toilet tissue, or pulling weeds in a flower bed.

Older children can assist with taking out the trash, mowing the lawn, sweeping the driveway, raking leaves, vacuuming shared living areas, dusting furniture, and mopping.

Even if you have hired household help, children need to learn basic cleaning skills so they can maintain their own homes some day.

Meal-Related Chores

In addition to helping with general housekeeping, every person in the family should have some responsibility for meal preparation, serving, or cleanup. Young children can tear up lettuce leaves and put them in a bowl. Older children can set the table, stir soup or gravy, pour beverages, clear the table after a meal, wash dishes, or put clean dishes away.

Cleanup Days

Major cleanup days are productive and can be fun—especially with the reward of a movie, pizza, or both at the day's end! Several such days might be designated each year. After all the trees have shed their leaves in autumn, "Final Raking Day" can be the day that leaves are removed from the yard. "Spring Cleaning Day" can be a day for deep-cleaning all draperies, upholstered furniture, carpets, and windows. "Closet Cleaning Day" can be a rainy-day activity for clearing out or sorting closets. "Garage Cleaning Day" can be a day for sorting items that have been temporarily stashed in the garage, and for making certain that all liquids (especially oils and antifreeze) have been safely stored. Make up your own special family cleaning days for your situation.

You may want to have an annual or biannual garage sale—clearing out unused items, and designating the money earned toward a family vacation or special event.

You can also use cleanup days as an opportunity to share some of your excess with a local charity.

Pet Care

Every family member should bear some responsibility for pets. Young children can put water in a puppy's dish. Older children can be taught to clean up after, feed, or bathe a pet. You may want to keep a pet-care chart for easy reference to make certain that pets are not overfed and that cages or fish tanks are cleaned on a regular basis.

Car Care

Periodically have a clean-out-the-car day with every member of the family helping. Remove the clutter in the interior, then thoroughly vacuum and clean the car from top to bottom, inside and out. Make this a fun, warm-weather family activity. (Splashing is allowed!)

Assign Chores

Keep a chore list available for consultation by family members, and with it keep a checklist so each person can indicate when a chore has been completed. This will build accountability. A chore assignment sheet can also help mediate family squabbles about who is expected to do what. Adjust chores from time to time so every person in your family has experience with a variety of chores. Some chores may be daily, others weekly.

To Reward or Not to Reward?

You should decide as a family which chores deserve to be rewarded. A number of child-development experts recommend a three-tier reward system:

• At least some chores should simply be expected of a child as part of family involvement—such chores are not linked to an allowance and are not rewarded. These chores give a child a sense of family involvement and responsibility. Praise and thanks is the only reward given.

• At least some family work opportunities should be made available to a child for extra spending money, above and beyond any allowance—such chores might be linked to a specific cleanup task, housekeeping chores, or laundry chores. Work opportunities should be made available for a child to earn extra money to apply toward a specific item. Remuneration should be based on the quantity of work or hours involved and how well the work has been done. Praise is also given as a reward. Some instruction may also be given to help a child complete the task at an even higher quality level in the future. This gives a child a sense of reward based upon effort and diligence.

• At least some chores should be done with the entire family and with a family reward at the end. This gives a child a sense of team effort.

Those who advocate this three-tier reward system usually suggest that a base allowance be given to a child simply as spending money, unassociated with tasks.

Working Together

Do chores with your child as often as possible. This gives you time together and an opportunity to teach your child how to do chores or make household repairs. It also gives you an opportunity to demonstrate a good work ethic. Even if you are cleaning out a cupboard while your child polishes silver, you can benefit by doing chores in close proximity to allow for conversation as you work. Your child will resent working while you sit and relax. On the other hand, your child will enjoy working if it can be done *with* you, especially if there is plenty of praise and thanks for his or her effort. This applies to teenagers as well as young children!

45 Develop a Family Health and Safety Plan

To be prepared for war is one of the most effectual means of preserving peace.

—GEORGE WASHINGTON

ALL PARENTS WORRY about the safety of their children. You can't always be with your children to protect them and help them make decisions, but you *can* teach them how to protect themselves.

Information Savvy

Teach your child to say his or her full name and age *clearly*, as well as to recite your address and phone number. Various jingles and songs can make this information easy to learn, even for toddlers. Also teach your children from early years to call 911 in case of an emergency—and *only* in an emergency.

Give your child swimming lessons as soon as he or she is able to walk. Teach your child basic safety rules associated with riding in automobiles (buckle the seatbelt), boats (wear a life vest), and hiking in the woods (keep a whistle on a string around your neck).

Basic Home Safety

Child proof any cabinets in which you store cleaning supplies, medicines, and other chemical substances that are potentially poisonous or dangerous to your child. Teach your child the serious consequences of inhaling or ingesting cleaners. Also teach your child the international warning signs for poison and high-voltage wires.

Label and store keys in a safe place, and never leave your car keys in the ignition, especially if a child is in the automobile.

Have sufficient locks on the doors and windows in your home. If you like to open windows at night, make sure you have closures that allow the window to be opened only enough for a breeze to enter, not a person.

Remove dangerous debris from your home and yard. Work with neighbors to clean up vacant lots near your home.

Consider installing a security system in your house.

Stranger Alert

Teach your children to be polite to strangers but never to take anything from them or go with them, regardless of what the person may offer. Make certain your children know each individual who has permission to pick them up from school. Have a secret password that only you, your children, and trusted friends know. In emergencies, your child can be assured that the person offering to transport her or gain entrance to the house has parental permission to do so.

If your neighborhood does not have an Alert Neighbors program, start one. Your local police department can help. The program provides training as well as signs for your neighborhood.

Emergency Supplies

Keep a supply of water, easy-to-open canned goods, paper products, and other basic items solely for emergencies. If you take any item from the storage area, be sure to replace it as soon as possible. Include among these items a flashlight or generator.

Basic First Aid

Keep an adequate first aid kit in your home and a second one in your automobile. Keep a chart handy that gives emergency first aid information should a child or adult be badly cut, ingest poison, lose consciousness, or have a seizure. Attend CPR (cardiac pulmonary resuscitation) classes as a family.

Fire Safety

Make certain you have sufficient working smoke alarms for your home. Teach your children the basic fire-safety rules: "Stop, drop, and roll." Have periodic fire drills with your family, choosing and rehearsing various escape routes depending on the location of the fictitious fire you assign to a fire drill. Train each child in what to do should smoke fill a room (crawl on hands and knees) or block a doorway.

Gun Safety

Make sure all guns in your home are locked in a cabinet, and that only parents know where the key is kept. Never store a loaded gun. Keep ammunition and guns in separate locked locations. Teach your children the basic gun-safety rules advocated by the National Rifle Association: "If you see a gun, stop. Don't touch. Leave the area. Call an adult."

Storm Safety

Every area of the United States is subject to one or more natural catastrophes. Before severe weather or an earthquake occurs, have a response plan. If you live in an area prone to hurricanes or tornadoes, designate a safe place in your home away from windows, if no storm shelter is available. Also, purchase a weather radio that tunes into emergency broadcasts involving severe weather and sends a wake-up or warning signal should storm warnings be issued. Know the differences between storm "watches" and "warnings," as well as the differences between siren warnings for floods and storms.

A Family Survival Plan

Develop a disaster-survival plan specifically for your family and drill it annually with your children. Make certain everybody knows where to go and what to do—as well as what to take with them should they leave the house. Designate a safe place where family members should meet once they have safely evacuated your house or neighborhood.

Environmental Safety

Choose to live in an area with the purest air, soil, and water possible. When purchasing a home, ask for an environmental report on the area and make certain the home is not near high-voltage wires. Consider purchasing new-technology air filters and a water filtration system for your home. Know if the area has flooded or been subject to forest fires in the past.

Babysitter Guides

Choose babysitters wisely. Make certain the babysitter is fully aware of all family emergency numbers and procedures. Stay in touch with your babysitter during your evening out or weekend away. If you have a daily babysitter or nanny, make certain that you have thoroughly screened this person against national registries for child abuse. As an added precaution, you may want to install hidden video cameras in your home so you can monitor childcare throughout the day.

Safe but Not Paranoid

Assure your child that the world is mostly a safe place, and most people can be trusted. At the same time, make certain your child is prepared for the places, times, and people who are not safe or trustworthy. A child who is forewarned and forearmed, with both information and sufficient practice in safety procedures, feels much more secure and confident. Parents who train their children in safety procedures and safeguard their homes as much as possible also feel more confident and secure.

46 Guard against Negative Influences

The quality of an individual is reflected in the standards they set for themselves.

—Ray Kroc

THE GOAL OF PLAYING hide-and-seek is not to hide so well that you cannot be found. Rather, it is to outwit the person seeking you and make your way to a designated spot, where you yell, "Home free!"

"I'm home free" was the daily statement made by one businessman as he returned home each evening. One day his daughter asked him, "Dad, why do you always say you are 'home free' when you walk in the door at night?"

He replied, "Because here at home I'm free of all the hassles, troubles, temptations, problems, and bad attitudes I've encountered out in the world. Here at home, I'm free to be loved and to rest and to feel secure and peaceful."

Is Your Home Free of Trouble?

The answer depends greatly upon the influences you as a parent allow inside your home. There are six main sources of outside input that invade the sanctuary of your home:

- television programs
- videos and DVDs
- music
- video games
- the internet
- printed materials (books and magazines)
- people

Do your best to make sure that each source of input is *positive*.

Monitor Your Media Input

It is the parents' right and responsibility to take charge of their children's media input.

- *Television viewing.* Make sure you know when and what your child is watching. Keep television sets in public rooms. If you allow your child to have a television set in his or her bedroom, you give up a great deal of control over what your child watches.

Limit viewing to no more than two hours a day, and seek to greatly reduce *that* amount of time. One family opted to allow their children to choose two hours a *week* of primetime television for viewing Monday through Friday, and then another two hours each weekend. Decisions were carefully made by parent and child once a week. The parent later said, "Our children learned a great deal about choices, compromise with their siblings, and they also acquired a criterion for what they knew would be acceptable viewing."

Whenever possible, sit with your child and watch the television programs you consider acceptable. Turn off the program if the values presented are contrary to those of your family. Discuss programs with your child. Help him or her develop a value-based criterion for determining if a program's message is helpful or harmful.

In discussing programs with your child, you can also help instill literary criticism—talk about the plot structure (or lack of a good plot), characterization (and the degree to which most characters are two-dimensional), and various techniques used to evoke emotions (such as music and camera angles).

Electronically block or unsubscribe to channels you do not want your child to watch.

- *Videos and DVDs.* Watch movies before you allow your child to watch them. Do not permit R-rated movies into your home, and carefully consider PG-13 movies, which often contain sexual content, violence, and offensive language.
- *Music.* Listen to a CD or read through its lyrics before you allow your child to purchase it. Go to a music store with your child as a regular outing! Encourage your child to explore a variety of musical styles. Listen to radio stations that are popular with young people. Discuss song lyrics with your child and place the same limitations on radio that you place on television. Be especially wary of lyrics that advocate sexual or violent behavior and rebellion against authority.
- *Video games.* Don't allow your child to play a video game for more than a half hour each day. Choose games that develop spatial and logic skills. Refuse to allow your child to play violent games, especially those that are highly graphic and involve hurting or killing human beings.
- *The internet.* Monitor your child's access to the internet, and block access to certain areas of the web. Teach your child good cyberethics. You'll find a discussion of topics like cyber ethics at www.cybercitizenship.org.
- *Print materials.* Don't allow pornography of any kind

into your home. Monitor closely the magazines and books your child reads. Suggest that your child read literary classics that have stood the test of time.

Know Your Child's Friends

Get to know the friends your child associates with at school, church, or in a social club. Converse with them. Volunteer to chaperone school events or be an aide in your child's school. See how your child interacts with various children and social groups. Also get to know the parents of your child's friends. Limit relationships that you believe have a negative influence on your child.

Be careful about who you invite into your home for overnight stays, social functions, or as dinner guests. If you do not want your children exposed to people who use offensive language; gossip about others; tell ethnic, racial, or sexual jokes; or advocate values and behaviors that you oppose, don't invite those people inside your home!

What You Take In Becomes Who You Are

The saying "You are what you eat" might be translated to other forms of input, such as, "You think about and act out what you see, hear, and read."

- *Violence begets violence.* Educational research of television and video games repeatedly shows that viewing excessive violence builds anger in children already prone to anger, and causes children who are not angry to feel less secure in their homes and neighborhoods. If your children encounter violence—especially on television, in movies, or as part of video games—discuss that violence with them.

- *Rebellion begets rebellion.* The more your child takes in messages that undermine authority and decency, the more likely he or she is to disobey rules and act in an uncivil manner toward others.

- *Exposure to sexual material begets desire for sexual stimulation.* It also results in a denigration of the opposite sex and devaluing of nonsexual affection. Help your child recognize that the consequences of sexual behavior are rarely represented on media programs.

47 Schedule One-on-One Time

Children spell "love" . . . T-I-M-E.

—Dr. Anthony P. Witham

TAKE TIME TO GET TO KNOW each member of your family. The best way to build relationships is to spend one-on-one time together. Do this on a regular basis. During your times together, focus on doing these things:

- *Make the other person feel special.* Introduce your child with pride to associates or acquaintances you may encounter. Dress and act in a way that won't embarrass your child (especially teens!). Show the same courtesies to your child that you show to an honored guest. Ask for his or her input, and give your child choices about things like menu and price range.

- *Make the other person feel like an important part of the family.* Point out ways in which the person has made a significant contribution to the family, and how much you appreciate his or her personality. Applaud ways you have seen the other person interact positively with others. Take this

time to praise the person's expression of values, kindness, responsibility, and compassion.
- *Make the other person feel involved with you.* Don't speak in general terms—get personal! Say how you feel about the person and express how much you enjoy spending time with him or her.

What Might You Do Together?

You don't need to set an appointment. Take events as they come. Some parent-child events may be connected to a school, scouting group, or service club. You might also consider these options:
- *Take your child to work with you.* Some companies sponsor annual "Bring Your Child to Work" days. Most companies also allow your child to come periodically as long as he or she does not disrupt the work flow or cause distractions. If a child's presence during the workday is inappropriate, most companies allow your child to visit your workplace on a weekend afternoon or after hours. Make sure you supervise your child, and remember that the purpose is to spend time *together.* Ask your child to help you do something productive and meaningful—perhaps filing or collating reports. Do not leave your child alone in an area with machinery or computers. If your child does meaningful work during an office visit, reward him or her appropriately.

If you have to make an out-of-town business trip, and your child is out of school, consider making the trip together. Find a special place for lunch or dinner. Share with your child the nature of your visit and what you hope to accomplish. Prepare your child for what he or she will do while you are with a client or company representative. One man has fond childhood memories of going with his father to check irrigation pumps after supper, and going out in the fall to bring in loaded cotton trailers. He has said, "Those were special times with Dad—just the two of us, being farmers together."

- *Go to special places together.* The special place might be a driving range, fishing pond, ballpark, bookstore, music shop, or the local zoo. Special memories are often associated with outings to places a child has never been. You might even find a special place that is unique to both of you.
- *Attend special events together.* One young woman has special memories of going to symphony concerts with her mother. She especially remembers concerts involving solo performances of the clarinet and piano—both of which were instruments she played. Consider taking your child to puppet shows, children's concerts and plays, family-friendly movies, ice skating performances, and horse shows. Your teenage son will probably enjoy boat or car shows. Your teenage daughter may enjoy a fashion show at a local department store or a ladies tea sponsored by a charitable organization.
- *Have dinner with your child.* This is a great opportunity to teach your child manners associated with fine dining. Go someplace appropriate to your child's age and food interests. A man noted, "One of the best memories I have of being with my father during my teen years was the time we went to a fish restaurant together and ordered whole lobsters. I had never even seen a lobster before. It was an experience that caused us to laugh together, and laughter opened up good conversation. We bonded over that lobster!"

Planned or Spontaneous?

Choose both types of one-on-one activities. Sometimes it's best to plan, especially if you want to prepare your child for things that might be encountered on the outing.

Other activities can be spontaneous. One man recalls with great pleasure the time he accompanied his father on an overnight trip to do some repairs on a rental property. How surprised he was the next day when his father woke him early and said, "Let's go fishing!" They took a boat out for deep-sea fishing, a memory that had lasting effects. Today, this man is looking for ways to surprise his two young sons with fun outings.

Let Your Child Choose

When in doubt, ask your child! Be open to your child's suggestions, remembering to ask while you have sufficient time to make plans and create a budget for the occasion. One young girl told her father she'd like to take a ferry to an island near where they lived. The father said, "It never dawned on me that my daughter even knew this island existed. I was amazed how much she knew about the island and how eager she was to ride a ferry boat."

Honor Your Child's Dreams and Opinions

As you spend time with your spouse or child, listen, listen, listen. One-on-one time with another member of the family is your opportunity to learn about that person—know what he or she thinks, feels, and dreams about doing. Don't jump in with your opinion. Hear the other person out first, and take time to reflect on what has been said.

Adjust to Changing Ages and Interests

Don't assume that the things your child enjoyed doing with you as a youngster will be the same things your child will enjoy doing with you as a teenager. Adjust to their growth, maturity, and current interests.

48 Redecorate Together

Home—that blessed word, which opens to the human heart the most perfect glimpse of Heaven, and helps to carry it thither, as on an angel's wings.

—Lydia M. Child

A CHILD'S FIRST EXPERIENCE at making decorating decisions usually comes during the holidays—helping trim the tree or finding the right place for the Hanukkah candle. Eventually children become more aware of their surroundings and want a say in what their home looks like.

Children of every age can voice opinions about changes in the common areas of the house and in their own rooms. The family room or den, the game room, or even a screened-in porch may be the most frequent hangouts for older children and teens. Find out what makes them comfortable or uncomfortable about the room and get their suggestions for change. Remind them that big-screen digital televisions with surround sound are *not* technically part of the decor.

Some children may be too young to voice an opinion, but when given an opportunity, older children will give you feedback, even if it's "No, no, no" or "Get real," which means no, no, and no.

While the last thing you want is a three-year-old wandering around with a paint tray, nearly every child can be included in some phase of the work process. Decorating kids' rooms also provides an opportunity for siblings to learn to work together and compromise. Children learn to swap labor and help one another.

When your child is involved in decorating her own room, she'll have a greater sense of ownership. Decorating the room together is a fun parent-child activity, and you can save a bundle in wallpaper and professional labor costs.

Compromise

Every child needs a space of his or her own. With a growing child and his changing interests, how does an economically minded parent design a room that will last for several years? One of the first things you should decide is how much input to let your child have. You should definitely listen to what kind of room he would like.

Show your child pictures of kids' rooms from magazines, decorating books, or web pages and ask her which ones she likes best, and why. Look for common themes and elements, such as bright or pale colors, or a particular character or theme. Gathering this information will be important in the compromise process. Considering the work and expense of redecorating, it's probably best *not* to compromise with her on some issues. For instance, she may plead for bright red carpet, but you may overrule her in favor of a neutral color that will outlast her changing interests.

Inventive but Inexpensive

There are many fun products and techniques available these days that will look great in your child's room. They are reasonably priced and, best of all, perfect for including your child in the painting process. Stencils, wallpaper borders, sponge or rag painting, and even chalkboard paint are easy to apply and fairly goof-proof. Kids can help paint by using sponging and ragging, which involve a blotting motion, to apply a contrasting color over a base of another color. Stenciling and block printing are also good techniques for kids. Practice first on a piece of poster board to work out the kinks. Create a sample to tape to the wall to see how well it will work in the room.

Other decorating ideas include jumbo stick-ups. These vinyl-like appliques can be reapplied many times and come in an assortment of designs. You and your child can have fun decorating without spending a fortune.

Follow a Theme

Theme rooms are often much easier to create than they look, and sometimes furniture can help develop the theme. Bunk beds, for instance, are similar to train berths! Develop the theme by painting walls in a pin-stripe grayish blue. Hot glue plastic train tracks to a wall (easy to remove by an adult) with toy train cars running along the track. Paint railroad-crossing signs on one wall. Use red bandanas as curtains and wooden train pieces as bookends! Paint a depot or train station on one wall. For those who prefer ready-made props, consider framing photos of train memorabilia. Use inexpensive, standard-size and poster frames. Train tracks can be hand painted as a border around the room.

Furniture Shopping

When picking out furniture, choose items that will grow with the child. Here are some other things you should consider:

- Opt for furniture that's more traditional. Your son may prefer the race-car-shaped bed, but he'll soon tire of it and you'll be forced to purchase a new one.
- Scout garage sales and want ads for bargains. You might actually find that race-car-shaped bed for a fraction of its new price. You can please your son now and still have enough money to purchase traditional furniture later.
- Make a headboard instead of buying one. Headboards are relatively simple to make, materials are inexpensive, and you can customize the look.
- Consider purchasing bunk or trundle beds. As a child grows, having the space for a friend to sleep over becomes more important.
- When purchasing a dresser, shelves, or desk, choose items with rounded edges. They could help avoid an injury.
- Use a good latex paint that will stand up to scrubbing. Keep in mind that special techniques such as ragging make incidental wall marks nearly invisible.
- You can tone down a child's fancy without vetoing their impractical ideas. For example, if your daughter wants to paint her room bright orange, paint one wall orange and the other three a neutral color.
- Use a bold color or trendy character motif in curtains or sheets, which are more easily replaced than paint or wallpaper.

If a small child really wants to paint, let him make some handprints on the wall. After they dry, paint the child's name underneath.

REDECORATE TOGETHER

49 Be an Encourager

To us, family means putting your arms around each other and being there.

—BARBARA BUSH

STRONG FAMILIES ENCOURAGE each other on a regular basis by expressing love and appreciation—especially when a family member does not feel deserving of those things. Communicating encouragement is even more important when children are barraged with messages of *conditional* love. Conditional love says a child is loved and accepted only *if* he or she is a certain weight, makes good grades, or gets on the right team.

In her book *52 Simple Ways to Encourage Others*, C. E. Rollins notes that the word "encourage" literally means to "INcourage, to plant courage into another person—and thus, to help endow him or her with the necessary elements and strength for facing the present and the future with boldness and confidence."[1]

Ways to Encourage Others

What are some things we can do to encourage others?

Be present. When times are especially challenging—death in the family, surgery for a loved one, a failed marriage—a person's quiet presence gives more strength than words can say.

If a child has been criticized, help her sort out the good from the bad of what was said to identify what is true and false. Not all criticism should be taken seriously, but some of it can be helpful as a learning experience. Instead of returning criticism to a teacher who says your child is not giving his schoolwork his best effort, take that seriously and help your child apply himself to his work. Encourage the child to learn from the assessment and develop an action plan to grow and overcome weaknesses.

On the other hand, if another child unfairly criticizes your child for taking an unpopular stand, help her see that she has a right to her opinion and convictions—and so does everyone else.

Mixed Blessings

Point out to your child that every person has strengths *and* weaknesses—we're all a mixed blessing. Be vulnerable to your child and share some of your own weaknesses, both as a child and an adult. If your child does not excel in athletics but has musical talent, help him find the area in which he can thrive. When you see steps taken toward improvement, encourage him to keep going forward. Notice even the smallest things that your child is doing well, and reinforce them with encouragement.

Words can sound empty and meaningless when your child

is facing a huge disappointment. Failures are real and they hurt. Don't take them lightly. Encouragement needs to be sincere to be effective. "You'll get over it" and "Tomorrow is another day" are clichés that don't heal a hurt. How about saying, "What can I do to help?" or "Do you want to talk about it?" When there are no words to be said, communicate encouragement with a hug, pat on the back, gentle touch, or kiss on the cheek. Those actions send the message that you care and want to be supportive.

Be Creative

Make a list of your child's strengths and the things you like about her—her smile, the way she cares about people, her responsibility in feeding the dog, her ability to make you laugh—then be sure to reinforce those good qualities when you see them in action.

Be creative in expressing encouragement. Say it in such a way that your child knows you have listened to him and you know his fears and anxieties. Encouragement is most effective when it comes from sincere people who know us well.

There are many ways to let people know how special they are. Leave a note on their pillow or in their book bag. Go for a long walk with that special person and express your appreciation for him or her. In *The Family Bond*, Dr. Susan Smith Kuczmarski suggests that a parent should view himself or herself as a child's "resource librarian," keeping a list of a child's accomplishments and achievements to encourage him when he has had an especially bad day.[2]

Three Steps to Encourage Others

In *Charting Your Family's Course,* educator and author Eric Buehrer outlines a three-step technique for encouraging others:[3]

1. First, identify what behavior was done. This makes the encouragement specific and more effective. Instead of a general comment like "You're such a great kid," say, "You did a great job keeping your room clean this week."

2. Second, comment on the character quality reflected by the behavior. This focuses attention on who the person is rather than on what was done. For instance, in addition to the above comment, say, "Thanks for taking the initiative to pick up your room."

3. Third, make a positive statement about the person's future. Let the child know that good character qualities will serve him well. For example, "Taking initiative will open doors for you in your future."

Everyone needs encouragement, and everyone can be an encourager. Just as a pebble dropped in a pond causes ripples all around, sincere praise and encouragement produce positive ripples into other parts of life.

50 Nurture One Another's Talents

My mother said to me, "If you become a soldier you'll be a general; if you become a monk, you'll end up as the pope." Instead, I became a painter and wound up as Picasso.

—Pablo Picasso

RECOGNIZE THAT NOT ALL MEMBERS of your family have equal talents or gifts—neither do they have the same desires or dreams. Find a way of nurturing the specific talents of each person without allowing the family schedule and resources to revolve around one person.

Allow your family members to pursue their unique gifts without projecting *your* desires or talents onto them. Don't expect your child to have the same talents you have. Don't expect your spouse to be good at, or like, all the things you enjoy.

In one family, Mom had a great interest in sports and had participated in athletic competition as a child. She wouldn't have dreamed of missing a college football game, and she still watches them on television whenever possible. On the other hand, Dad was adept at singing and had worked his way through college by singing in a barbershop quartet. He never went to a football game his entire four years at college! Today the entire family watches football games together, both live and on television. They also go to concerts together. On more than one Saturday, they have gone to a football game during the day and a concert at night. Both children in the family have participated in competitive sports; they've also taken music lessons and performed in choirs and orchestras.

Individual Activities but Family Involvement

A mother of four children once noted, "Kurt is into baseball, Katie is into dance, Kiersti is into horseback riding, and Keith is into basketball. We have no trouble deciding what to do for fun as a family—we simply go as a family to watch the games, performances, or special practices of each child in turn. Kurt knows ballet from jazz dancing, Kiersti is good at detailed baseball stats, Keith knows equestrian scoring, and Katie knows just the cheer to give for a free throw. If one or more of the kids is bored with watching a particular lesson or practice, I let them go to a nearby supervised area to play games among themselves." Rather than letting their children move alone in different directions, this family opted to have the entire family move in four directions simultaneously.

As the children grew older, Kurt was able to drive Kiersti to morning riding lessons and Katie took dance classes in the same gym where Keith played off-season basketball pickup games. The family enjoyed going to competitive dance recitals, games, and meets, sometimes with Dad taking one child in one direction while Mom and another child went another way. As often as possible they turned out-of-town competitions into opportunities for family fun—perhaps by visiting a zoo, amusement park, beach, or museum in addition to the competitive activity.

Expose Your Child to a Variety of Activities

For a child to know what he enjoys and is good at doing, he must be exposed to a variety of activities. Let your child attend summer camps. These often are made available by cities, churches, or schools on a free or low-cost basis. Seek out free clinics or school clubs that can expose your child to an activity prior to investing in equipment or lessons.

Choose mental activities (chess club, spelling bee competition) as well as physical activities (hiking, swimming). Choose team activities (soccer, dramatic performance) as well as individual activities (writing, photography).

Give Your Child an Opportunity to Develop Skills

Once your child identifies a particular area of interest, help her develop skills in that area. Tutoring or lessons may be the best way to go. Start with a limited number of lessons, while being sure to provide adequate training so your child can see progress in her skills. Insist that your child commit to regular practice for any activity in which you are required to invest money for lessons or equipment.

Limit the number of interests that your child simultaneously pursues. Perhaps limit your athletic child to one sport per semester, or two sports per year. You might also couple an athletic activity (ballet class) with a mental activity (acting class).

Give your child an opportunity to help pay for his own lessons, special equipment, or attendance at a clinic or camp. You might match what your child contributes—perhaps dollar for dollar, or even ten dollars of your own for each dollar a child contributes. If a child is helping to pay for lessons or equipment, he is far more likely to practice, take care of equipment, and take his involvement in an activity seriously.

You and other families might hire an expert to teach a group of your children. This is especially good for painting, cooking, or etiquette classes. Such classes can include children of a variety of ages and abilities.

Encourage Your Child to Use His or Her Skills

Encourage your child to use newly developed skills in a way that benefits others. If your child is interested in singing, encourage him to sing in a choir or ensemble group, especially one that performs for those with limited exposure to music (such as residents of a nursing home or children in a hospital).

Not all skill-development activities require lessons or out-of-pocket expense. For example, if your child expresses an interest in nursing, check into the opportunities for her to become a candy striper or other form of volunteer at a local hospital.

Be Your Child's Biggest Fan

As a parent, you automatically become your child's number one fan. Teach your children to become fans in support of their siblings. Remember these basic rules about being a parent fan:

- Root for the entire team or performance group, not just your child.
- Be supportive of the coach or instructor and his or her decisions. Don't insist that your child play every minute of every game or be in every dance number of the recital.

- Know the basic rules of the game or event. Don't embarrass your child with your ignorance.
- Don't coach from the stands or audience. Save any tips or suggestions on your child's performance for another time and place.
- Don't criticize referees, umpires, or judges, either during a competition or after. Your criticism will upset your child and rarely make a difference in the officiating, the fairness of judging, or the ultimate score.
- Let your child know that you are proud of the way he played or performed. If he did well, acknowledge his good performance. If he made mistakes, let him know that *you* know he can do better and believe he *will* do better in future outings, and that you love him nonetheless for showing up and giving his best effort.
- Show good sportsmanship to parents of children on both your child's team and the opposing team.

Acknowledge and praise your child's display of good sportsmanship or efforts to boost team morale. Acknowledge that it takes courage to perform under public scrutiny and evaluation.

APPENDIX: A Reflective Test for Parents

Here is a short self-assessment quiz for parents. It's a quick way to understand how well you know your child. Answer honestly, but don't be discouraged if your answers aren't always what you think they should be. Use this quiz as an opportunity to learn new ways to love and support your child.

- Can I name my child's three best friends?
- Do I know my child's goals?
- Am I physically active with my child (shooting hoops, jogging, etc.)?
- Do I make dinner for my family?
- Do I talk to my child about managing money?
- Do I spend thirty minutes of one-on-one time with my child every day doing something we both enjoy?
- Do I talk to other parents about raising kids?
- Do I talk to other parents specifically about raising sons or daughters?
- Do I base restrictions for my child's activities on his or her gender?

- Do I talk to my child about media messages?
- Do I tell my child what his or her strengths are?
- Do I know what school project my child is working on?
- Do I view pornographic material?
- Do I participate in parenting organizations?
- Do I yell at my spouse?
- When I converse with my child, does he or she do most of the talking?
- Do I know what my child is concerned about today?
- Have I read my child's school's sexual harassment policy?
- Do I help boys learn to respect girls, and vice versa?
- Do I tell my child stories about my own youth?
- Do I volunteer to help with my child's extracurricular activities?
- Do I take my child to school?
- Have I ever visited my child's school during the day?
- Do I take my child to work with me?

For parents who live away from their children:

- Do I initiate contact with my child at least five times a week?
- Do I ask how my child feels about transitioning to and from my home?
- Do I demonstrate respect for my child's other parent and stepparent(s)?
- Do I fulfill my visitation and support commitments?

Endnotes

CHAPTER 1
1. Irene Franck and David Brownstone, *The Parent's Desk Reference* (New York: Prentice Hall, 1991), 126–127.
2. Laurene Johnson and Georglyn Rosenfeld, *Divorced Kids* (New York: Fawcett, 1992): excerpted in *The Family Matters Handbook* (Nashville, TN: Thomas Nelson, 1994), 285–295.

CHAPTER 2
1. Susan Smith Kuczmarski, *The Family Bond: Inspiring Tips for Creating a Closer Family* (Lincolnwood, IL: Contemporary Books, 2000), 99–100.
2. Kathryn Hirsh-Pasek, *How Babies Talk* (New York: E. P. Dutton, 1999).
3. Peter L. Benson, *The Troubled Journey: A Portrait of 6th–12th Grade Youth* (Minneapolis: Search Institute, 1993), 84.
4. *Robert F. Kennedy Memorial*, <http://www.rfkmemorial.org/RFK>.
5. Kuczmarski, *The Family Bond*, 102.

CHAPTER 3
1. J. K. Kiecolt-Glaser, W. B. Malarkey, M. A. Chee, T. Newton, J. T. Cacioppo, H. Y. Mao, and R. Glaser, "Negative Behavior During Marital Conflict Is Associated with Immunological Down-Regulation," *Psychosomatic Medicine* 55 (1993): 395–409.

CHAPTER 6
1. Sharon Merhalski, "Family Tradition of Loving Others—Teaching Selflessness," *Titus2Women*, <http://www.titus2women.com/Articles/SharonMerhalski/MomSense/Unselfishness/PrinterFriendly.shtml>.
2. Jana Fortner, "Tackle 'Mine-it is.'. . .," *The Lexington Herald-Leader*, April 9, 2002.

CHAPTER 8
1. Photo preservation information from Susan Otto, Photo Archivist, Milwaukee Public Museum (from http://www.nlg.dk/preservtext.html).

CHAPTER 9
1. Linda and Richard Eyre, *Teaching Your Children Values* (New York: Fireside, 1993), 24.

CHAPTER 10
1. Paul Faulkner, "Hugs and Kisses," *Heartlight* <http://www.heartlight.org/articles/200002/20000209_family1259.html>.
2. Ibid.

CHAPTER 13
1. Dolores Curran, *Traits of a Healthy Family* (New York: Ballantine Books, 1983), 132.
2. Robert Putnam, *Bowling Alone: The Collapse and Revival of American Community* (New York: Simon and Schuster, 2000), 101.

CHAPTER 15
1. Larry Christenson, quoted in William Mitchell, *Building Strong Families* (Nashville, TN: Broadman & Holman, 1997), 41–43.

CHAPTER 16
1. "Ten Tips for Talking with Kids about Tough Issues," *Talk with Your Kids*, <http://www.talkingwithkids.org/first.html> (20 April 2002).
2. Ibid.

CHAPTER 17
1. Charles F. Stanley, *Experiencing Forgiveness* (Nashville, TN: Thomas Nelson, 1996), 72–76.

CHAPTER 25
1. A variety of tests are discussed in *Tests: A Comprehensive Reference for Assessments in Psychology, Education, and Business*, edited by Richard C. Sweetland and Daniel J. Keyser (Kansas City, MO: Test Corporation of America, 1986).

CHAPTER 26
1. Dorothy Strickland, "Meeting the Needs of Families in Family Literacy Programs," *Family Literacy: Directions in Research and Implications for Practice*, January 1996, <http://www.ed.gov/pubs/FamLit/need.html>.

CHAPTER 27
1. "CASA Announces Family Day—A Day to Eat Dinner with Your Children," *The National Center on Addiction and Substance Abuse at Columbia University*, <http://www.casacolumbia.org/newsletter1457/newsletter_show.htm?doc_id=82442>.

CHAPTER 30
1. Thomas Cole, *The Journey of Life: A Cultural History of Aging in America* (Cambridge: Cambridge University Press, 1992), xix.

CHAPTER 38
1. Dave Ramsey, *Financial Peace* (New York: Viking, 1995).

CHAPTER 42
1. Jack Barr, "Indebted to Education," *Case Currents*, January 2000 <http://www.case.org/currents/2000/January/tpoints.cfm>.

CHAPTER 43
1. Mitchell, *Building Strong Families*, 69–91.

CHAPTER 49
1. C. E. Rollins, *52 Simple Ways to Encourage Others* (Nashville, TN: Thomas Nelson, 1992), 1.
2. Kuczmarski, *The Family Bond*, 65–66.
3. Eric Buehrer, *Charting Your Family's Course* (Wheaton, IL: Victor, 1994), 109–110.

Popular Books by Starburst Publishers®

50 Ways to Stand Up for™ Your Family: Build a Legacy of Love for Everyday Living
By W. B. Freeman

    American democracy depends on healthy families to produce responsible citizens. Learn how to strengthen your family with heart-warming anecdotes, how-to advice, interesting historical information, and practical tips. Be inspired to rediscover your nuclear and extended family's culture, traditions, and pass the benefits of family to your children and grandchildren.
(trade paper)   ISBN 1892016745   **$11.99**

50 Ways to Stand Up for™ America: Put the Spirit of July 4th into Everyday Life
By W. B. Freeman

    Rev up your patriotic spirit with heart-warming anecdotes, how-to advice, interesting historical information, and practical tips. Learn flag flying etiquette. Discover the benefits and responsibilities of good citizenship. Be inspired to take part in your community, and find that one-for-all-and-all-for-one attitude. Make the spirit of July 4th relevant for everyday life.
(trade paper)   ISBN 1892016702   **$11.99**

Cheap Talk with the Frugal Friends
By Angie Zalewski and Deana Ricks

    A collection of savvy tips and tricks for stretching the family dollar from the celebrity thrifters known as the Frugal Friends by their radio and television audiences. This book is packed with money-saving tips on various topics including automotive, beauty care, cleaning products, dating, decorating, entertainment, medicine, pet care, and sporting goods.
(trade paper)   ISBN 1892016583   **$9.99**

Incredible KidEdibles
By Beth Brigham
> Discover over 125 recipes for easy-to-make critters, airplanes, and boats. Make unforgettable party snacks, tasty art projects, memorable holiday treats, and edible doughs. Each recipe is illustrated to help you craft magic for and with kids. Create a snack and a smile.
> (trade paper)   ISBN 1892016451   **$12.99**

The Little Inspirational™ Bathroom Bible™ Book
By W. B. Freeman
> Bathroom reading is different. You're looking for a short read– a little humor, some inspiration, or encouragement. This book gives you all of this, plus trivia, quizzes, and heart-warming stories. It's filled with lots of information that's rated "G"– for the Good Book.
> (trade paper)   ISBN 1892016680   **$13.99**

The End-Times Survival Handbook: What to Expect before the Rapture and What to Do about It Now
By Joan Hake Robie and Daymond Duck
> Nobody knows the future, but the Bible does shed light on current and future events. This handbook is packed with survival tips to help you defend your faith and family, identify false prophets, and be a responsible prayer warrior. Understand the importance of history, prophecy, and the work of the Holy Spirit. Learn to comfort, edify, teach the truth, and warn others about the end times.
> (trade paper)   ISBN   1892016729   **$13.99**

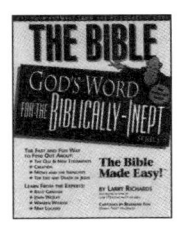

The Bible–God's Word for the Biblically-Inept™
By Larry Richards

An excellent book to start learning the entire Bible. Get the basics or the in-depth information you seek with this user-friendly overview. From Creation to Christ to the Millennium, learning the Bible has never been easier. The best-selling *God's Word for the Biblically-Inept*™ series mixes scholarly information from experts with helpful icons, illustrations, sidebars, and timelines.
(trade paper)   ISBN 0914984551   **$16.95**

Revelation–God's Word for the Biblically-Inept™
By Daymond R. Duck

End-time Bible prophecy expert Daymond R. Duck leads readers verse by verse through one of the Bible's most confusing books. Follow the experts as they explain the captivating prophecies of Revelation and point out related current events! Over 100,000 sold!
(trade paper)   ISBN 0914984985   **$16.95**

Revelation for Teens: Learn the Word™
Unwrap the mysteries of Revelation in this Biblically-Inept™ brand of simplified Bible commentaries for teens. Don't sweat the future. Learn everything God wants you to know about what's going to happen, including the Rapture, the Tribulation, the Antichrist, and the new heaven and earth. New features, including "Happenings" and "Stop," are combined with popular elements from the adult series, such as "Key Symbols," definitions, illustrations, and study questions.
(trade paper)   ISBN 1892016559   **$14.99**

Don't Miss These Popular Web Sites!

www.biblicallyinept.com
www.sundayschoolteach.com
www.homeschoolteach.com
www.learntheword.com

Purchasing Information

www.starburstpublishers.com

Books are available from your favorite bookstore, either from current stock or special order. To assist bookstores in locating your selection, be sure to give title, author, and ISBN. If unable to purchase from a bookstore, you may order direct from STARBURST PUBLISHERS. When ordering please enclose full payment plus shipping and handling as follows:

Post Office (4th class)
$4.00 with a purchase of up to $20.00
$5.00 ($20.01–$50.00)
9% of purchase price for purchases of $50.01 and up

Canada and Overseas
To be determined by destination

United Parcel Service (UPS)
$5.00 (up to $20.00)
$7.00 ($20.01–$50.00)
12% ($50.01 and up)

Payment in U.S. funds only. Please allow two to four weeks minimum for delivery by USPS (longer for overseas and Canada). Allow two to seven working days for delivery by UPS. Make checks payable to and mail to:

Starburst Publishers®
P.O. Box 4123
Lancaster, PA 17604

Credit card orders may be placed by calling 1-800-441-1456, Mon.–Fri., 8:30 A.M. to 5:30 P.M. Eastern Standard Time. Prices are subject to change without notice. For a catalog send a 9 x 12 self-addressed envelope with four first-class stamps.